Culture, Indigenous Knowledge and Development in Africa:
Reviving Interconnections for Sustainable Development

Munyaradzi Mawere

Langaa Research & Publishing CIG
Mankon, Bamenda

Publisher
Langaa RPCIG
Langaa Research & Publishing Common Initiative Group
P.O. Box 902 Mankon
Bamenda
North West Region
Cameroon
Langaagrp@gmail.com
www.langaa-rpcig.net

Distributed in and outside N. America by African Books Collective
orders@africanbookscollective.com
www.africanbookcollective.com

ISBN: 9956-791-91-1

DISCLAIMER
All views expressed in this publication are those of the author and do not necessarily reflect the views of Langaa RPCIG.

Dedication

To all the people of Africa

Table of Contents

Acknowledgements

I would like to thank Prof Francis Nyamnjoh and Dr Artwell Nhemachena for the rich discussions we often had at the University of Cape Town around issues that affect Africa and the African people. The discussions were indeed useful in helping me reflecting on some of the themes that run throughout this book. I am grateful also to Pedro Jovo for his meticulous reading of the manuscript and offering helpful suggestions. The Managing Editor of Langaa RPCIG, Dr Roselyne Jua has supported me in all my work in ways too numerous to mention. May the Most High God bless you all!

Preface

The interconnections between culture, indigenous knowledge, and development in Africa cannot be underestimated: it should not only be acknowledged but fortified if sustainable development on the continent is to be ever realised. The question of sustainable development is critical as it is one at the core of all forms of development that one can imagine, from human to economic development, from social to political and environmental development. This means that the present book is not only critical but comes at the right time – a time when the talk on sustainable development as achieved through the bolstering of the interdependence between culture, indigenous knowledge (IK) (or what Semali and Kincheloe (1999: 37) call subjugated knowledge), and development is high on the agenda of the African continent. At a global level, a key moment marking the significance of IK in development can be traced back to the United Nations Conference and Development (UNCED) held in Rio de Janeiro, Brazil in June 1992. At this conference, the need to develop mechanisms to protect the earth's biodiversity was stressed. Many of the documents signed at UNCED[1] also reflect the requirement to conserve the knowledge of the environment that is possessed by many local communities (IK) with the resultant Agenda 21 being the starting point for sustainable development calling for major efforts to be directed to the recording of indigenous knowledge. Following this crucial event was the IDRC[2] sponsored International Conference on "Indigenous Knowledge and Sustainable Development" held in September 1992 in Silang, Philippines. This conference was the first major international manifestation and promotion of IK among the development community. Since then, the development community's conception of knowledge which was always influenced primarily by the philosophy and methods of Western science shifted towards the local community, that is, knowledge by the [indigenous] people and for the people in question. Davies and Ebbe[3] aptly captured this in their foreword to the proceedings of the Conference on Traditional Knowledge and Sustainable Development held in support of the United Nations Year of the World's Indigenous People by World Bank in September 1993 when they said: "Few, outside of some anthropologists and historians recognised that there are myriad sciences embedded in cultures of other peoples and civilisations throughout the world. Today, both scholars and public policy makers are recognising the importance of various local or culture-based knowledge systems in addressing the pressing problems of development and the environment".

All these events, followed later by the June 1997 Global Knowledge Conference held in Toronto, emphasised the urgent need for the global world to learn, preserve, and exchange indigenous knowledge with the developing countries as both contributors to and users of knowledge. Such an appreciation of the value of indigenous knowledge was contrary to the long standing tradition of European education and scholars of discrediting and trying to eradicate all forms of knowledge that were non-European by origin. This was on the realisation that [local] knowledge, not capital, is the key and basic component for sustainable social and economic development of any country or society. Besides, there was a growing consensus among scholars, development agencies, and policy makers that knowledge exchange must be a two way street: a sort of conveyor belt moving back and forth as one directional movement of knowledge from the rich developed countries to the poor developing ones was seen to have failed and causing resentment on the part of the recipients. As pointed out by Semali and Kincheloe (1999), since the 1960s Eurocentric scholars have begun realising the importance of indigenous knowledge especially its economic contribution to the global market. Even in his call for a new inclusive approach to development, the then President of the World Bank, James D. Wolfensohn[4], stressed the need for a framework that deals inter alia with indigenous people and their knowledge. In the context of the Partnership for Information and Communication Technology for Africa (PICTA), the World Bank agreed to lead an Indigenous Knowledge for Development Initiative to help stimulate recognition, utilisation, and exchange of indigenous knowledge within and between communities in the development process.

While it is over two decades now after some important strides have been made at global level to accommodate and integrate IK for development, nothing much has changed: the pace at which IK is being integrated for development across the globe is not only slow but disheartening. It is out of this observation and realisation that a book such as this was born to further push for the recognition and fostering of the interconnections and relationships that have always existed between culture, indigenous knowledge (IK) and [sustainable] development especially in Africa. While many scholars have looked at the problems associated with IKs in post-colonial Africa, this book makes a difference in that it goes beyond exploring the problems by emphasising the need for reviving interconnections between culture, IKs and development across the continent. Besides, the book departs from standard treatments in IKs discourse by attempting to demystify the long standing myths and dangerous assumptions by many Eurocentric scholars and missionaries that the indigenous people of Africa had no science, worse still the notion of development. To achieve this, I have captured several case studies of indigenous knowledge systems across the continent and demonstrate that if these IKs are carefully integrated into the mainstream development discourse, they can go a long way in promoting sustainable development and lives of many on the continent and beyond.

On the same stroke, this book is a formidable challenge to Eurocentric scholarship and Western science fundamentalism that due to the long standing influence of Western imperialism have come to believe that Western science is the only answer to development and all other problems that face humanity across the world. Yet, I quickly underscore that the present book does not only challenge fundamentalism of one kind – Western science fundamentalism – but fundamentalism of all kinds including [African] IK fundamentalism; otherwise the book would be a substitution of Western science fundamentalism with fundamentalism of another form. To avoid falling prey to fundamentalism of any kind, I employ in my argument and analysis Mignolo[5] and Grosfoguel's[6] concept of critical border thinking – a concept with which they critique both imperial fundamentalism and fundamentalism of the subaltern – in my critique of Western science. Using the concept of critical border thinking, I argue that for sustainable community development or at least human development at community level to be achieved, there is need to find better ways to learn about indigenous institutions and practices and where necessary adapt modern [scientific] techniques (i.e. 'global best practices') to the local practices. Thus in Africa, Western knowledge is only rendered relevant to the local community needs when the indigenous knowledge fails or at least as a complement of indigenous knowledge; hence the book is also a call for a sustainable dialogue between different forms of knowledge for sustainable development. The book is a valuable asset for policy makers, institutional planners, practitioners and students of social/cultural anthropology, education, science studies, development studies, African studies, heritage studies, and political/social ecology.

Chapter 1

Culture, Indigenous Knowledge, and Development in Africa: Exploring the Interconnections

This chapter, as partly with the focus of the book as a whole, is a broad interrogation of the intricate interconnections and relationships between culture, indigenous knowledge and development in Africa. The interconnections and relationships between culture, indigenous knowledge and development in Africa cannot be underestimated: they are recognised and will continue to be recognised for quite some time especially by the rural community members who largely depend on [African] indigenous knowledges (or what I call African sciences) in their everyday life. I underscore that the impact of these interconnections and relationships determine the continent's direction in terms of sustainable development and economic, socio-political freedom. Before delving much into the examination of the interconnections, it is of utmost importance to unpack the concepts 'culture', 'indigenous knowledge' and 'development' separately and in line with the purpose of this book. This is important as more often than not, the aforementioned concepts are elusive.

Understanding culture

Etymologically, the concept of culture is derived from the Latin word *cultura* stemming from *colere* meaning "to cultivate" (Bastian 2009). However, the concept and definition of culture is hard to pin down such that it has been well documented in literature, and scholars have provided a number of interpretations to the term. As I argued elsewhere (Mawere 2010: 146), "the complexity of coming up with a universally agreed definition of culture is predicted by the fact that social problems differ from society to society, and this tend to define the role that culture has to play in society as well as the expectations of society on how and to what extent culture should help solving economic and socio-political problems".

The lack of a specific and universally agreed definition of culture has met with serious repercussions. It has resulted in the vulnerability and confliction interpretation of culture by different scholars across disciplines. Alfred Kroeber and Clyde Kluckhohn (1952), for instance, compiled a list of 164 definitions of culture prompting many other scholars to formulate and conjure up broad definitions for culture describing it with different terms such as basic assumptions, feelings, canons, values, behaviour, and so forth (Benedict 1959; Sapir 1991; Hall 1992; Schein 1992; Trompenaars 1994). Benedict (1959), for instance, defines culture as the canons of choice, that is, the principles that allow people to make choices in their lives. Kluckhohn and Strodbeck (1961) introduce the concept of value orientations or points of references to explain the phenomenon of culture. Sapir (1977) suggests that culture is a silent language because different cultures present dissimilar perceptions about time, space, ownership, friendship and agreements. And, for Schein (1992: 97), culture is a pattern of shared assumptions that a group of people learned as it solved its problems of external adaptation and internal integration that has worked well enough to be considered valid and, therefore, to be taught to new members as the correct way to perceive, think and feel in relation to those problems. Similarly, Trompenaars (1994) proposes that culture directs people's actions. He observes that culture is man-made, confirmed by others, conventionalised and passed on for younger people or new comers to learn. This connotes that for Trompenaars, as with Benedict and Schein, culture is more of a compass that provides people with a meaningful context in which to meet, to think about themselves and others, and to face the outer world. Van der Walt holds almost a similar understanding of culture to the one enunciated by Trompenaars and others. For him (1997:8), "culture is not only something alive: It is rich and complex as it includes habits, customs and social organisation, technology, language, norms, values, beliefs and much more". This implies that culture always exists where people exist.

As I have elaborated elsewhere (Mawere 2010), I should underscore the point that, though the concept of culture has been interpreted differently throughout history, as has been revealed in many of the definitions of culture above, what cuts across a number of definitions that scholars have provided on the concept is the general belief that culture is most commonly used and understood in three basic senses:

♦ As an integrated pattern of human knowledge, belief and behaviour that depends upon the capacity for symbolic thought and social learning.
♦ As the shared attitudes, values, goals and practices that characterises an institution, organisation or group.
♦ As excellence of taste in the fine arts and humanities, also known as high culture.

The three senses elaborated above captures the different definitions that have been attributed to the concept of culture over the years. They also show that culture (civilisation) is a product and creation of a people (see also Vilakazi 1999; Ntuli 1999) which means that all communities – whether rural, urban or semi-urban – have certain traditional knowing innovations, norms and values that can be considered as culture. In this respect, I argue with Frantz Fanon (1967, 1968) that culture is opposed to custom. In actual terms, I argue that "culture is living and changing (or dynamic), while custom is reified, formal and rigid" (see also Gibson 2011: 54). Besides, the three senses explicated above underline the fact that the definition of culture is indeed elusive. In view of the [three] senses elaborated above, and for purposes of this book, culture shall be understood as an integrated pattern of human knowledge, beliefs, behaviour, values, attitudes, goals and practices that characterises an institution, organisation or group of people. The fundamental idea of culture, thus, is that it reflects both the social imperatives and the social consequences of human behaviour (in a given society) in their interaction and conduct among themselves and with members of other societies.

Indigenous knowledge

The concept of indigenous knowledge is a combination of two terms, 'indigenous' and 'knowledge' that should be separately unpacked before analysing it wholesomely. To start with, the term 'indigenous' literally mean original, first, native to a place or aboriginal people to an area. And, the term knowledge, if to be understood generally without delving into the philosophical sophistications around it could be

4

understood as a personal belief that is somehow justified and with the capacity to influence one's thinking, action and behaviour. Since the present book is not a venture into philosophy in general and epistemology in particular where I might be obliged to unpack in philosophical terms the concept of knowledge, the general understanding of knowledge given above suffice to show what knowledge is generally all about. I will, therefore, right away move on to examine the concept of indigenous knowledge as a whole.

In terms of the definition for 'indigenous knowledge' as a concept, quite a number of them have been proffered by scholars across disciplines that have indigenous knowledge as one of their objects of study. These include social/cultural anthropology, cultural studies and sociology, among others. Yet I should underline that given the fact that we cannot sensibly talk of IK without mentioning indigenous knowledge systems (IKSs) from which the former derives its meaning, in this book, the terms (IKS) and indigenous knowledge (IK) are applied to mean one and the same thing, and therefore used interchangeably. In Africa, IKs have always been used to sustain human life and that of the environment since the beginning of history of humanity on the continent to advance the needs and aspirations of the society in question. This suggests that IKs are quite enduring and dynamic such that they have survived the test of time and history. In view of this understanding, IKs have been conceived as local knowledge(s) that is unique to a given culture or society (see http://www.sedac.ciesin.columbia.edu website). They [indigenous knowledges] are "the information bases for a society which facilitate communication and decision-making, and are continually influenced by internal creativity and experimentation as well as by contact with external systems"

5

(Flavier *et al.* 1995: 479). IKs are also understood as knowledge forms that have failed to die despite the racial and colonial onslaughts that they have suffered at the hands of Western imperialism and arrogance (Altieri 1995). These three definitions suggest that IK as a form of knowledge is intergenerational, that is, it is passed on from one generation to another by those who hold it such as the elders in a society. Also worth noting from the definitions given above is that IKs have originated naturally and locally in a particular society or from a particular group of people. However, a critical question that remains difficult to answer is: 'What does it mean to be local?' In relation to the definition proffered by Altieri, another question arises: 'Does IKs as knowledge forms only exist in formerly colonised areas?' Considering these two mind boggling questions, my conception of IKs or IKSs identifies with Ocholla who perceives IKS as "a complex set of knowledge and technologies existing and developed around specific conditions of populations and communities indigenous to a particular geographic area" (Ocholla 2007: 2). I should point out here that the complexity of IKS results from the logical qualification with the word 'system' as it suggests generations of creative thought and practice as well as a network and 'meshwork' of processes with different components such as knowledge, belief and technology. Also, IKs are 'indigenous' because the meanings as well as the categories of sense making are deeply context-bound in so far as they are generated internally within a cultural community and are/were produced through 'indigenous' thinking or exploration whether material, philosophical, religious or linguistic that was inspired by the group's needs, creativity, and aspirations. This means indigenous knowledge can also be understood (if you like) as local knowledge (Warren 1991; Kargbo 2005), traditional knowledge, local technical knowledge, indigenous and traditional knowledge (Sillitoe 1998; Kawooya 2006), community knowledge, folkloric knowledge (Sillitoe 1998; Kargbo 2005) and in some cases, also known as subjugated knowledge or alternatives to knowledge produced within the boundaries of Western science (Semali and Kincheloe 1999: 37). Warren (1992) captures this aptly when he asserts that the term indigenous knowledge (IK) is used synonymously with 'traditional' and 'local' knowledge to differentiate the knowledge developed by a community (indigenous people) from the international knowledge system sometimes also called 'Western' system, generated through universities or the academy, government research centres and private industry. In Zimbabwe, they would call such knowledge as IK *"ruzivo rwevana vevhu"* (literally: *knowledge of the children of the soil*) which means knowledge of the people with African origin. *Vana vevhu* (children of the soil) therefore do not only mean people of Zimbabwean origin but can also be referred to mean people of the African origin as all these people have special relationships with the African land: African land is the land where their *mikuvhute* [singular: *rukuvhute in Shona*](umbilical cords) as well as their ancestors were buried. As can be seen, what commonly underlies all these bodies of knowledge known as IKs is the fact that they are developed through the processes of acculturation and through kinship relationships that societal groups form, and are handed down to posterity through oral tradition as well as cultural practices such as rituals and rites. As such, IK is resilient: it remains the adhesive or epoxy resin that binds and harmonises society as it constitutes communicative processes through which

7

knowledge, beliefs, customs and moral values are transmitted, preserved and acquired by members of a given society (Mawere 2010). Emphasising the resilience of indigenous knowledge, Shizha (2010: 28), for example, observed that "indigenous knowledges are known for their resilience and ability to describe, explain, predict and negotiate nature".

At this juncture, it is of utmost importance to highlight that just like many other concepts across disciplines, indigenous knowledge as a concept has been problematised over the years as scholars tried to come up with a precise understanding of what it means to say knowledge is indigenous. What many scholars have generally agreed without much debate and disagreement are the important tenets of indigenous knowledge that:

♦ It is embedded in a people's culture as it is manifested in the community's collective history, beliefs, practices and relationships.

♦ It is collective though some parts of it are sacred and secrete to a group or some individuals.

♦It is holistic in so far as it contains a total worldview.

♦It is never static, but always dynamic. This is in view of the fact that no human being and consequently society is an island unto itself. It is in fact well known that human beings are by nature social and *zoon politikon* (to use Aristotle's terms).

In fact IK covers all facets of human society such as natural resources, socio-economic and political relations, agriculture, engineering, language, religion, art and so on. In short, indigenous knowledge (or indigenous knowledge systems as I use them interchangeably in this book) includes plant biology, environmental education, and other education centred activities such as manufacturing, agriculture, food processing, civil engineering, animal husbandry, transportation, mining, communication (Snively and Corsilglia 2001), oral, ecological and spiritual knowledge. This is what scholars like Warren (1991: 1) also allude to when he says:

> *Indigenous knowledge is the local knowledge — knowledge that is unique to a given culture or society. IK contrasts with the international knowledge system generated by universities, research institutions and private firms. It is the basis for local-level decision making in agriculture, health care, food preparation, education, natural-resource management, and a host of other activities in rural communities.*

♦ It is the basis of modern knowledge systems.

♦ It is part of the global heritage that needs to be recognised for the common good.

In fact as given in literature elaborated above, and in particular by Ellen and Harris (1996) and later the World Bank (1998: 2), the special features of IK could be summarised as below:

♦ IK is local in that it is rooted in a particular community and situated within broader cultural traditions; it is a set of experiences generated by people living in those communities. Separating the technical from the non-technical, the rational from the non-rational could be problematic. Therefore, when transferred to other places, there is a potential risk of dislocating IK.

♦ IK is tacit knowledge and, therefore, not easily codifiable.

♦ IK is transmitted orally, or through imitation and demonstration. Codifying it may lead to the loss of some of its properties.

♦ IK is experiential rather than theoretical knowledge. Experience and trial and error, tested in the rigorous laboratory of survival of local communities constantly reinforce IK.

♦ IK is learned through repetition, which is a defining characteristic of tradition even when new knowledge is added. Repetition aids in the retention and reinforcement of IK.

♦ IK is constantly changing, being produced as well as reproduced, discovered as well as lost; though it is often perceived by external observers as being somewhat static.

Yet before laying to rest my discussion of how IK has been conceptualised over the years, I should underscore that while external observers, especially those still holding on to colonialist ideologies who argue from a Euro-American perspective, and some scholars who understand IK as a commodity located and found out there [in the rural areas] have argued that IK is "static" (Hountondji 1997) or "immovable" (Turnbull 2000), I argue otherwise. I argue that this perception based on the commodification of IK is narrow and derogatory: it excludes the perspective of the knowledge producers; hence it requires serious revision. Also, arguing from the perspective of the IK producers (e.g. African people), I assert that IK just like other forms of knowledge such as Western science is never static. Neither is it immovable. This is because IK is dynamic and continues to develop as new challenges in the society arise: it continually evolves and adapts itself in response to gradual changes and demands in the social and natural environments given that it is closely interconnected with the community's cultural values and passed on from one generation to another sometimes with modifications. Besides, IK can be exchanged or transferred from one community to another: in the production of indigenous knowledge, societies can influence one another (influence others while being influenced as well) as communities interact (social constructivism) such that to label indigenous knowledge as static or immovable is a misnomer or rather opprobrious. In fact as has been emphasised by scholars such as Blakeney (1999) and Chavunduka (1994), while terms associated with indigenous knowledge such as "traditional" might suggest that such knowledge is old and static, the reality is that IKs are dynamic forms of knowledge that are constantly changing in accordance with the need and development of concerned societies over time. Marie Battiste (2002: 33) also aptly captures this when she observes that Eurocentric scholars have taken three main approaches to indigenous knowledge in Africa. First, they have attempted to pejoratively reduce indigenous knowledge to taxonomic categories that are always static over time, and as a body of old information that has been handed down essentially unchanged to posterity. Second, they have deliberately tried to reduce indigenous knowledges to their quantifiably observable elements, that is, to what can be seen, touched and experimented of these indigenous knowledges. Third, Eurocentric scholars have mistakenly assumed that indigenous knowledge has no validity in the physical world except in the metaphysical or spiritual realm. I argue with Battiste that none of these three approaches to indigenous knowledge adequately captures and explain the holistic scope and nature of indigenous

11

knowledges as understood from the perspective of their producers and users. Besides, none of the three approaches pays adequate attention to the role and importance of indigenous knowledge to people of the communities where the IKs originate and even to other communities where IKs could be transferred: they seem to misunderstand the fact that indigenous knowledge is not indigenous because it is static but because it is linked to a particular social group which can be identified in a particular setting [geographical location] at a particular time. In this sense, the geographical location need not only be African but could also be American, European as all forms of knowledge (whether Western or African) are locally-produced ethnoknowledges; hence the shortfalls of Hountondji and Turnbull's characterisation of indigenous knowledge elaborated above.

Development

While *Development Studies* as a degree programme has been proliferated in many universities across the globe, what *development* really is has remained contested: it has been understood differently by scholars across (and even within the same) disciplines. Amartya Sen (1999), for instance, has seen what he calls 'real development' as a process that should free all humankind "that lay everywhere in chains although born free" (to use Jean Jacques Rousseau's words). It should be emphasised that Sen's understanding of development was much linked to economics as a discipline, and in particular to the history of the rise of capitalism which he saw as a limiting factor to other people's freedom. It is this capitalism that Karl Marx (1859/1977) also saw in his: *A contribution to the critique of political economy* as a shattering force for human freedom and dignity. Sen's understanding of development, thus, could be conceived in economic terms. Yet since the 1970s, there was general consensus among scholars that there was more to development than economics such that it would not be proper to define or understand development only in economic terms (Dei 2002; UNESCO 2006). There was realisation that besides economic factors, there were many other factors that affect the trends and patterns of development of a particular society such as culture, political systems, and social systems, among others. With this realisation, many other definitions of development were postulated. This is one reason why scholars such as Thomas (2004:1- 2) has considered "development' as a concept which is contested both theoretically and politically, and is inherently both complex and ambiguous". The controversy and complexity of 'development' emanates from the fact that development encompasses many variables that all need to be seriously considered.

Having realised this, the 1996 United Nations Development Programme emphasises development as specifically related to humankind – what it [the programme] calls "human development," measured by life expectancy, adult literacy, access to all three levels of education (primary, secondary and tertiary), as well as people's average income, which is a necessary condition of their freedom of choice. In a broader sense, the notion of human development incorporates all aspects of individuals' well-being, from their health status to their economic and political freedom. According to the Human Development Report (1996: 10), published by the United Nations Development Programme, "human development is the end and economic growth a means. So, the purpose of growth should be to enrich people's lives". This means that the standard of living of all people should be high to avoid a situation in capitalistic societies where the standard of living of people could be poor in the midst of plenty. This is not to say that economic growth by way of increasing a nation's total wealth doesn't enhance the potential to reduce or even eradicate poverty and other socio-political problems that haunt humanity. The argument, however, is that there are many examples of nations in the world whose economic growth were never followed by human development in terms of improving their quality of life. In fact, many nations that have gone through capitalism such as Britain and America (and closer home, South Africa) have witnessed a great deal of human suffering (instead of life improvement) in the name of development resulting in scholars such as Frantz Fanon, Steve Biko and Karl Marx, among others, criticising capitalism and all its tenets. Put differently, in many capitalistic societies, economic growth was achieved at a great cost of human suffering, inequality, high unemployment rates, high pollution levels, environmental degradation, industrial diseases, weakened democracy, loss of cultural identity, or overconsumption of natural resources needed by future generations (see also Human Development Report 1996). This means the structure and quality of growth is indeed an issue for 'real' development or what I consider in this book as 'sustainable development'. For these reasons, many development experts and scholars have now generally agreed that economic growth that negatively impact on humanity and the environment in general is inevitably unsustainable, that is, it is temporal in so far as it cannot continue in the same line for long a time: such economic growth yields no positive results to the common majority. I can take the example of pollution that results from economic growth through industrialisation. Such growth is inevitably unsustainable as sooner or later it may appear that even more resources would be required to deal with the pollution problem which in any case has the potential of provoking other serious problems such as those to do with human healthy. Thus in the long run, the growth causes more suffering than it improves human lives and life of the environment (or ecosystems) in general. There is no sustainability, therefore, no sustainable development in such economic growth. We may need to briefly explain what we mean by sustainable development to determine why it is more important to promote sustainable development than it is to promote economic development alone.

Sustainable development is a term that is widely used by scholars and policy makers all over the world, yet its understanding still lacks a uniform or universally agreed interpretation. Though widely acknowledged as an important concept in world politics and developmental issues, the concept of sustainable development is, thus, still in the process of constant definition and re-definition. However, a working definition of the concept, "sustainable development" (also known as the Brundtland Report) has been given by the World Commission on Environment and Development (1987: 43) as development that "meets the needs of the present without compromising the ability of future generations to meet their own needs." As can be seen, this definition contains within it two key concepts:

♦ *the concept of* **needs***, in particular the essential needs of the poor people in the world whose needs should be prioritised; and*

♦ *the idea of* **limitations** *or the* **imperative to control** *technology and social organisations that are potentially threatening to the* *environment's ability to meet the needs of the present and future generations.*

These two key concepts above suggest that all definitions of sustainable development require that the world be understood as a system with different structures connected to each other through time and space.

While the classical definition of sustainable development given by WCED (1987) is quite convincing, perhaps a critical question that remains unanswered is whether such development is practically achievable or else it remains forever an idea that never ceases to be imagined.

The nexus between IK, culture and development: Where and when IKs are used for development?

While prior to the world war two, the Western world especially Britain and subsequently the United States of America had widely spread the conception (generally considered as Western models of modernisation) that development could be explained in purely economic terms, this was challenged by many scholars after the Second World War. Though many scholars (particularly those with capitalistic ideas) from the Western world have continued to hold on to the misconception perpetuated by America and Europe, since the 1970s "some consensus seems to have emerged that development could not be measured and implemented in purely economic terms only" (Kotze 1984: 9). This consensus was reached on the realisation that some correspondence was necessary between development and culture. Galtung (1970), for instance, observed in the 1970s that the establishment of complicated technological projects in countries without the supporting educational facilities and infrastructure by some development agents would not be rightfully considered as development (as the American and British conceptions dictated before world war two) but mere implementation of a particular project. There was need to consider the social as well, especially issues to do with culture and other such values. Mervyn Caxton (cited in Eade 2002: xii-xiii) puts this neatly when he observes that "[all] models of development are essentially cultural" as they derive from particular cultures. This means that development is a cultural construct and of course the basis for inter-cultural engagement, though in most cases on unequal terms. The centrality of culture for development is further captured in Caxton's (cited in Eade 2002: xii-xiii) observation that:

> *When a people faces challenges from the environment which require responses and solutions, one of the functions of culture is to provide criteria which would enable a selection to be made between alternative solutions. This essential role of culture is usurped, and its capacity to provide adequate responses to development challenges is impaired, if the criteria used are ones that are external to the culture itself. This is what happens when external development models are exclusively relied upon.*

The need for consideration of culture in issues of development came out of the realisation by theorists of the interconnections existent between the economic, social, political, and cultural aspects of technology though they [theorists] did not move a step forward to explore the nature of interdependence (Kotze 1984). According to the World Development Report (1998: 3, emphasis original):

17

Knowledge [whose basis is culture], not capital, is the key to sustainable social and economic development. Building on local knowledge, the basic component of any country's knowledge system, is the first step to mobilise such capital. Moreover, there is a growing consensus that knowledge exchange must be a two way street. A vision of knowledge transfer as a sort of conveyor belt moving in one direction from the rich, industrialised countries to poor, developing ones is likely to lead to failure and resentment

Similar sentiments were pronounced by Joseph Stiglitz (1998), Vice President and Chief Economist of the World Bank, when he noted:

Governments and international institutions can certainly help countries with the daunting task of sifting through international experience, extracting relevant knowledge and experimenting with it. But they will have the most success if they help developing countries adapt knowledge to local conditions. Sharing knowledge with the poor is most effective when we also solicit knowledge from them about their needs and circumstances.

In more or less the same way, Odora-Hoppers (2001:1) have argued that indigenous knowledge is "embedded in the cultural web and history of a people including their civilisation and forms the backbone of the social, economic, scientific and technological identity of such a people". Similar sentiments have been echoed by Vandana Shiva (Cited in Ishemo 2002:35) who has carefully noted that:

All societies have "*ways of knowing*" and "*ways of doing*" and that... *all societies, in all their diversity, have had science and technology systems on which their distinct and diverse development has been based. Technologies or systems of technologies bridge the gap between nature's resources and human needs. Systems of knowledge and culture provide the perception and utilisation of natural resources.*

This entails that the need to engage local communities and local government, as opposed to the Western models of modernisation which ignored the local, was for the first time in history realised not only by intellectuals but also by some international development agencies such as the World Bank. Indigenous knowledge (IK) as imbedded in culture became central in steering and fostering development that aim to benefit the poor directly as it was now realised that IKs are normally used to design and implement projects for development in marginalised societies or those societies where knowledge from modern sources is scarce or inapplicable.

It should be noted first and foremost that it is development in the Western sense that relegated IK through its modernisation theory founded in positivistic scientific methodologies that viewed IK as superstitious, illegitimate, primitive, and unscientific. Yet where [African] IK is given the opportunity to steer development, it could be as efficient as or even more efficient than Western science in certain contexts, for example, where certain forms of 'development' could result in adverse health, socio-economic or political results such as industrial diseases, pollution, economic inequality, inflation, retrenchment, and subjugation of some groups in a given society. No wonder why some Western programmes imposed on Africa have failed (and are still failing). Green revolution is a case in point. When it was introduced to Africa, the assumption was that Westerners knew what the indigenous Africans want and that what the latter wanted is what the Westerners themselves already have. The planners of the programme, therefore, did not put into account the perspectives of the Africans and Africa (where the programme was being implemented) leading to its dismal failure in the African continent. The same has been experienced with policies such as the imposed International Monetary Fund (IMF)/World Bank's Structural Adjustment Programmes (SAPs) in the late 1980s and early 1990s in many African countries such as Mozambique, South Africa, Zimbabwe, Zambia and others. Talking of the impact of ESAP in Zimbabwe, for instance, Richard Saunders (1996: 8) notes:

> *The initial economic shock treatment undertaken with ESAP's launch in the early 1990s hit the business sector and ordinary Zimbabweans very hard, and.... price control relaxation saw inflation explode and consumer demand shrink, by as much as 30 %...with deeper and systemic problems in the 'reformed' economy, including high inflation (which has stubbornly remained above 20 %, averaging 28.8% in 1991 – 94, instead of falling to the projected 10 %) and a continued substantial government deficit (which has fluctuated around 10 %, averaging 8.8 % of GDP in the early 1990s, far above the 5 % level anticipated by the World Bank in 1990....The Zimbabwe Congress of Trade Unions estimated that about 55,000 jobs were lost up to 1995.*

In post-apartheid South Africa, when ESAP was launched in 1993, no significant improvement on the national economy and poverty levels was made. According to the Economist Intelligence Unit (1998: 41), the South African rand fell from levels of R3,65: $1 during most of 1995, to R4: $1 in March

1996. By mid-December the currency was trading at R4,7: $1, therefore having depreciated by 30% against the US dollar during 1996.

In conservation of the environment and natural resources, the Westerners, since colonialism in Africa have made the same blunder of applying those methodologies they deemed scientific relegating those of the local communities which they labelled superstitious, illegitimate, primitive, and unscientific. In many African countries, this has resulted in resistance by local communities resulting in land degradation, poaching and over-exploitation of many other natural resources – disasters which could have been avoided had indigenous people and their knowledge were seriously considered by settlers and external development agencies. As World Bank (2002; 2004) noted, IK has so far shown areas for development including environmental management, education, natural resource management, agriculture, healthy, medicine, gender equality, conflict resolution, and food security. Thus I argue with World Bank (1998: 7) that:

> *A greater awareness of the important role that IK can play in the development process is likely to help preserve valuable skills, technologies, artefacts, and problem solving strategies among the local communities. Often such local practices also have an impact on issues of global concern. Therefore, preserving the IK capital can enrich the global community and contribute to promoting the cultural dimension of development. In some cases it can also help to protect the global environment,*

To conclude this chapter, I underscore the point that the interconnections or relationships between culture, IK and development must be deliberately forged (where they have been destroyed or weakened as in many African societies) and in fact regularly fortified through crafting policy management that favourably foster sustainable development through acknowledgement of the value of culture is central to all forms of development.

Chapter 2

Culture, indigenous knowledge and development in Africa since colonialism: The silenced narrative

Culture contains indigenous knowledge of a people: it is the springboard of all humanity. Yet in Africa, culture has been despised by European settlers and missionaries for a long time now. This has been perpetuated by Euro-centric scholars. Yet, it is now generally agreed by many African scholars (and other critical scholars beyond the African boundaries) that with the advent of colonialism in Africa, the African cultures and indigenous knowledges were *unjustifiably* and *unfairly* despised and relegated as superstitious, primitive, illegitimate, irrational and unscientific. Shizha (2013: 4), makes a similar point when he argues that "African culture has been invaded by Western belief systems, ways of knowing, and ways of experiencing the world thus reinforcing the colonisation of African indigenous knowledges". And as Franzt Fanon (1967: 217) reminds us, "the lack of culture of the Negroes, as proclaimed by colonialism ought logically to lead to the exaltation of cultural manifestations which are not simply national but continental, and extremely racial". Now, given that development of any society largely depends on the culture and indigenous knowledges imbedded therein, the development hopes of Africa were apparently shattered prompting scholars such as Walter Rodney to publish his famous book: "*How Europe underdeveloped Africa*". It is this African story which I describe in this book as the silenced narrative: a narrative that was silenced by the European hegemonic colonialists and continues to experience the same through works of Euro-centric scholars and neo-imperialists. Before interrogating this silenced narrative, let us explore how African cultures and indigenous knowledges were traditionally known to be like before colonial administration sets roots in Africa.

Background to the African cultures and IKs before colonialism: Why culture and IKs matter?

The worldview of any group of people is shaped by their culture and knowledge systems embedded therein. So is development. This understanding helps readers to appreciate that as long as Africa had its own culture before its contact with Europe, the latter had its own knowledge systems that helped to shape and promote its own civilisations and development, be it economic, social, or political. This, however, should not be interpreted to mean that African cultures were and are homogeneous except that they share, among themselves, a lot in common than they do with Western cultures. Conception of ubuntu – a philosophy of humanness that embrace unity, love and peace –, for example, is pervasive and ubiquitous in many African cultures, from the southern to the northern and from the eastern to the western parts of the continent. As Ikuenobe (1999) reminds us, while there are many cultures existent in Africa, it is of uttermost importance to note that whenever a *'thought'* or *'tradition'* is predicated of Africa it does not connote homogeneity of cultures though similarities and convergences can be noted across these cultures. Instead, it is only making reference to dominant themes on the continent in terms of common generative themes across [African] cultures. It is in view of this understanding that, in this book, I talk of African culture(s). Granted, African cultures, indigenous knowledge and technologies before colonialism were not as diluted as they are today though they shared (or exchanged) with each other among themselves. This means that while there were differences between different groups of people or cultures, there were also many similarities between cultures across Africa. I confirm, for example, that there are inherent similarities between Bantu groups such as the Xhosa and Zulu of South Africa, the Ndau and Tsonga of Mozambique, the Shona and Ndebele of Zimbabwe, the Tswana of Botswana, and what Father Placide Tempels (1945), a Belgian missionary, noted about the Shaba Baluba of Congo in west Africa. Just to show the parallels between the aforementioned Bantu groups and the Shaba Baluba of West Africa, both talk of their spirit (*mweya* in Shona and Ndau of Zimbabwe and Mozambique) being happy, troubled, and low or having their spirit revived which is similar to what Tempels captures as *force vitale*, that is, vital force or soul. Also, important to note is that both the people of West Africa and sub-Saharan Africa had (and continue to have) their indigenous knowledges imbedded in their respective cultures. These knowledges were basically transmitted or passed on from one generation to the other through oral tradition, rites, ceremonies, and other such practices. Through these knowledges, innovations were made and problems of all kinds varying from health, economic, environmental, political or social were solved. While in many instances, problems and challenges in the community were perceived as a curse from the ancestors or works of witchcraft, they [problems or challenges] were also perceived as calls for new innovations, solutions and even critical thinking as long as that responded to the problems or challenges at hand. The innovations and thinking, however, always had their traces in the culture concerned. This means that Africans had a pragmatic epistemology as well as practical metaphysics with which they used to judge the worthiness of an idea, belief or explanation whether it works or not. This is why in many African societies, a belief, idea or explanation could pass as knowledge, and hence acceptable as long as it can solve the problems at hand. This is different from the Western understanding of reality which is totally based on objectivity and empirical validation. It is thus, through this different conception (from the Westerners) of reality that Africans understood the world, responded to the problems affected them, and related with each other and other groups as well as the environment around them. It should be stressed that this difference does not render African knowledge inferior to Western knowledge as it [African knowledge] worked for the communities that produced and employed it in their everyday life. Stressing the same point, Meki Nzewi (2007:7) argues through Touma that:

> *If our ancestors had no sound intellectual mettle, how did they develop the scientific cultures of food, childbirth and mental nurture, also the musical arts genres that were non-sanctionable mediators in the indigenous societal polity and social-cultural practices, including the policing of egalitarian law and order, medical arts delivery, etc.?*

The preceding discussion connotes that the original African people always had strong memories of their local practices, self-consciousness and consciousness of the other (or of the world around them). Through these memories, they mastered different skills to adapt and change local practices in order to suit the changing cultural, political, and socio-economic needs of their immediate environment. All the positive changes adapted were integrated gradually into the beliefs or knowledge systems and culture of the indigenous people concerned. It is from observations such as these that the World Bank (1998: i, emphasis original) made the remark that: "Indigenous knowledge provides the basis for problem-solving strategies for local communities, especially the poor *and the formerly marginalised.* It represents an important component of global knowledge on development issues". Yet indigenous knowledge remains an underutilised resource in the development process of rural communities in many African countries where [external] development agencies participate in issues of development. This is in spite of calls by some scholars and development experts that learning from indigenous knowledge, particularly by investigating first what local communities know and have has the great potential to "improve understanding of local conditions and provide a productive context for activities designed to help the communities" (World Bank 1998: i). One may therefore wonder why there is some sort of resistance or reluctance to pay heed to such an important call. It appears the seed of colonialism on Africa has done great damage not only to the African cultures and peoples, but also to those who dehumanised themselves by participating in the nefarious project of colonialism. In the next section, I focus on colonialism and how it impacted the African cultures, [African] indigenous knowledge and development.

Colonialism and how it impacted the African cultures, indigenous knowledge and development

The protracted slavery and colonial relationship between Africa and Europe resulted in the dehumanisation of the African people and perpetuated socio-economic, racial and cultural stereotypes about Africa and the [indigenous] African people. Africa was not only viewed by European imperialists as a dark continent but also seen as "a land of despotic civilisations with no legacy of those democratic principles that have been so clear to the West's self-image" (Mengara 2001:1). It is, therefore, out of the slavery and colonial encounter between Europe and Africa that led to what Mudimbe (1988) calls the "invention of Africa" (or what I call here a European defined Africa) as opposed to the Africans' Africa (that is Africa defined by Africans), based on caricature, misrepresentation, and the negative characterisation of Africa founded on the Aristotelian paradigms of a series of binary oppositions that seek to establish Western hegemony over Africa. Aristotelian categorisation of Africa has resulted in what Mengara (2001: 2) calls "the systematic and systemic manufacturing of a continent – *Africa* –" classifying it vis-a-vis Europe on the basis of "inferiority versus superiority, uncivilised versus civilised, pre-logical versus logical, mythical versus scientific, among other epithets". Just to give a more clearer example: It is an undeniable fact that while Eurocentric scholars have taken so much time to theorise concepts that seem to exclude or disadvantage Westerners such as 'indigenous knowledge', 'indigenous', and 'local' among others, to the best of my knowledge none of these scholars has seriously considered the theorisation of colonially constructed stereotypes for example around the issue of skin colour, in particular the concepts of 'white' versus 'black'. The concepts coined by Eurocentric theorists such as 'Whites' and 'Blacks' to refer to Europeans and African people who in terms of skin colour I consider as 'red' or pink and 'chocolate' or brown respectively, have remained untheorised simply because the former colonialists remain on the advantage – they [former colonialists) are comfortable when the chocolate skin people are referred to as Blacks and the red skin people are referred to as Whites. This is regardless of the fact that the concepts 'White people' and 'Black people' were coined by Eurocentric theorists to popularise the superiority and inferiority complexities or myths of European colonialists and Africans respectively and above all to advance the sole interests of the European imperialists. I argue that such concepts and many others that continue to privilege Europeans and should be deconstructed and reconstructed if de-colonial scholarship and theorisation is to be honestly executed and appreciated. While it could be argued that this is not only the Eurocentric scholars who have the obligation to reverse such stereotypes, the argument remains that it is them who created the stereotypes and so should bear responsibility and take the lead in the deconstruction of such stereotypical concepts they themselves created if what they (together with former colonialists) referred to as decolonisation is to be conceived as decolonisation in good faith. My personal experiences and observations (through reading and contact) over the years have been that in many cases Eurocentric scholars do not theorise concrete issues that directly affect the formerly marginalised (or the formerly colonised) on the African continent such as citizenship, bondage of national boundaries, poverty, skin colour, continued unequal distribution of land and other such resources between indigenous Africans and former colonisers (as in the case of post-apartheid South Africa) etc., but on those that affect the former colonisers or perpetuate the latter's continued domination over Africa and the indigenous African peoples. Worse still, many Eurocentric scholars continue imposing their theories on Africa – theories that the scholars designed to 'catch' Africans that they [Africans] remain trapped and deeply entrenched in the circle of poverty and problems of all kinds. What Africa requires are theories that help to solve concrete problems that have affected them since slavery and colonialism in Africa and that indeed continue to haunt them even today: theories that do not betray others but promote peace and harmony in the world. In view of this realisation and my aforementioned observations, I contend that even today such stereotypes, misrepresentations and prejudices against Africa and the [indigenous] African people have continued to be circulated and recycled by many Eurocentric scholars and African protégées (especially the brainwashed and the first crop of African Christian scholars) who are (or were) reluctant to critically reflect on the 'real' facts about Africa. Africa, thus, has always been dragged into problems by Eurocentric theorists since the dawn of colonialism on the continent.

As Mengara (2001: 2) observed, the grand trouble of Africa started on the Berlin conference of 1885 that yielded the 'scramble for Africa', to own the territory or the African land on the basis of the following circumstances:

♦ *The European empire's long attested desire to own portions of the world as a way of signifying their hegemonic grandeur.*

♦ *The transfer of their secular European rivalries onto virgin grounds where imperial wars could be indirectly fought; and*

♦ *A capitalist fervour that the colonial 'discoveries" of rich lands in Africa and America, the slave trade and the development of commerce with the Eastern and middle Eastern worlds had helped to trigger.*

The Berlin conference thus saw the domination and subjugation of Africa and the African people (especially their socio-political and economic freedom) as colonialism officially set in. This means that before independence in the 1960s and 1980s in Africa, all state sectors, from health to education, national economies to agriculture, and industry to politics, were run by the White minority who saw themselves as superior to all the indigenous African people. It is in this light that in colonial Zimbabwe, as elsewhere on the African continent, African culture, indigenous knowledge, traditional medicine, and all other things with the tug 'African' were despised and relegated to the periphery if not totally obliterated. As Ntuli (1999: 188, emphasis original) argues, this parochial and narrow "view of considering anything non-European as inferior *and useless* was based on the misconception that Western cultural knowledge orientations were used to determine the value of blacks' ideas, belief systems and religion". Goduka (2000) echoes the same sentiments when he argues that with the advent of colonialism in Africa the African indigenous values, beliefs and practices that did not conform to European norms were considered odious and repugnant. On the same stroke, Bhebe (2000: 7-8) blames colonialism as the major evil force that denigrated and hindered African creativity, science and technological advancement when he notes:

Before the European conquest of Africa, Africans had built up a pool of knowledge and technology which they used to sustain agriculture, human and animal health, industrial production involving food processing, metallurgy, leather tanning, timber seasoning, fermentation of beverages, making of dyes, mining and architectural engineering. But political subjugation by Europe so traumatised Africans that many of them lost confidence in and looked down upon their own culture, forcing some of them to view and embrace Christianity and Islam as a progressive move but without totally losing their old cosmology or basic beliefs.

Reflecting on pre-colonial indigenous knowledge systems and life in Africa in general as well as the changes that took place after the advent of colonialism, Nzewi (2007: 56) captures this poetically when he says:

> *Then --*
> *When there was spiritual enlightenment*
> *We were condemned for practicing humanness*
> *Humans lived in manageable groups*
> *Respecting cohered individualities*
> *The principle of life was "ubuntu" – we-ness*
> *Communalism coerced egalitarian longings*
> *Live and respect other's lives resolved conflicts*
> *And human musical arts healed injured minds.*

> *Now –*
> *When there is material enlightenment*
> *We have been commandeered into practicing modernism*
> *Humans live in amorphous geopolitics*
> *Dissonance stresses bonding rites*
> *Communalism is supplanted by selfism – me-ness*

Democracy enslaves the masses
Let us live and destroy them perpetuates conflicts
And plastic musical arts disable human-mindedness

On the same stroke, Daniel Mengara vehemently criticised and shamed the enlightenment scholars such as Immanuel Kant, Georg Hegel, Levy-Bruhl and others in formulating racist theories about the African people as a people that:

♦ *Had no history; therefore, they could not claim to know themselves and had to be told who they were by Europeans.*

♦ *Were cultural children shaped by sexual lust, immorality and degeneration?*

♦ *Could not rule themselves because of their primitive irresponsibility; therefore, they needed enlightened masters to show them the ways of superior civilisation and deliver them from ignorance.*

♦ *Could not claim ownership of Africa, or even of their lands since they were incapable of cultivating and managing them.*

♦ *Had no right to human justice, being sub-humans as they were.*

♦ *Had no religion and therefore needed the light of Christianity if they were to be freed from their chaotic state of nature and from animism (see Mengara 2001: 6).*

It is out of observations and reflections such as these captured in this book that renowned Africologist, Molefe Kete Asante (in Mengara 2001: xiv) argues that "Europe's intervention in Africa [was] the beginning of the most nefarious images. An African invented for European purposes could no longer serve the interests of its own

33

people" as Europe demonised and relegated to oblivion all that was considered African. Nzewi (2007:4) puts this well when he argues: "Irreverent and irresponsible abandonment as well as flippant change started when the human and cultural practices of the invaders from outside began to make insidious intrusions into the Africans' human and cultural psyche". I should underline that this relegation of the African culture and other indigenous values and practices by Europe was evident in all facets of life of the African societies that suffered Euro-colonialism. Writing of education during colonialism in Africa, Wa Thiongo (1986: 7), for instance, had this to say:

> *Colonial education [in Africa] was far from giving people the confidence in their ability and capacities to overcome obstacles or to become masters of the laws governing external nature as human beings and tends to make them feel their inadequacies and their inability to do anything about the conditions of their lives.*

Similar sentiments were captured by Waite (2000: 235, emphasis original) who on writing about medicine in Zimbabwe, had this to say of the White minority government during the colonial era that:

> *The health service was white-run* [with only Western medicine used], *white-staffed and practiced apartheid. It served the white minority and only incidentally ministered to the Africans, who comprised some 97% of the population. The white settlers, who controlled the colonial legislature, saw to it that they alone enjoyed posh medical attention.*

In the area of medicine in Zimbabwe (as in many other countries in Africa such as South Africa), the relegation of all that was associated with the indigenous African people was aggravated by the Witchcraft Suppression Act of 1899 which was passed to criminalise both malpractice and legitimate practice of traditional healers. This is because the Witchcraft Suppression Act subsumed most of the materials used by traditional healers, including all their charms and medicines they used to cure diseases, under the tag 'witchcraft'. Even herbal medicines were considered superstitious and unscientific and, with a few notable exceptions (Harvey 1962; Wild and Gelfand 1959). Such a move was meant to outmanoeuvre and outcompete traditional healers as the missionaries of the time wanted to promote their own Western-based medicines. They knew that as long as people continued relying on traditional healers and their medicines which were normally offered for free or at a very low cost, their [the missionaries] medicines would never find acceptance in Africa. As Chavunduka (1982) argues, the other implication of the Witchcraft Suppression Act is that it removed control of witchcraft accusations from traditional courts, assuming that the whole practice of witchcraft was a charade and a sham, [with] no real existence at all. From the perspective of the indigenous Africans, the Act put the colonial government in a very comprising position, that of identifying itself as an accomplice in the perpetration of evil in the African society. Witchcraft suppression Act of 1889 that was put in place by the White settler's regime, thus, could be viewed as a form of witchcraft itself considering the suffering of the innocent people that ensued from the Act.

I should reiterate that in such a harsh hegemonic and discriminatory environment where not only the medicines of the indigenous people were despised; the African cultures and indigenous knowledge imbedded in them were maligned and subdued, development staggered, and socio-economic and political ambitions shattered. Molefe Kete Asante (2001: xiii) aptly captures this when he argues: "At the top of the twentieth century Africa remains the most misunderstood of all continents, crippled in our imagination by images rooted in the minds of imperial Europeans who attempted to shape and invent an Africa useful to their political ambitions". Europe used its hegemonic power to subjugate Africa, to shatter Africa's knowledge production processes; yet it is well known that knowledge production processes are central to development of any human society. Obbo's (2006:154) captures this well in her observation that "as ever, power is key to ownership of the knowledge production process. Contemporary problems of development, health and indigenous knowledge demand that we define the theoretical agendas and practical issues that are of concern to us". The assumption by the European colonialists was that Africa was a *tabula rasa* (that is, a continent with no rationality and civilisation) before its contact with Europe, and that Western cultural systems of knowledge were the only means to be used in determining the value of Africa's ideas, beliefs and general way of life (Ntuli 1999). Even at school, indigenous Africans were defined as inferior to Europeans and were erroneously taught to internalise the racial stereotypes of the coloniser (Mazrui 1993). This negatively impacted on the indigenous African people's voice, self-identity, and self-esteem which instead of being enhanced were in fact were eroded during the schooling process. It is in this sense that some chief advocates of indigenous knowledge (Agrawal 1995a, 1995b; Battiste 2002; Cassie 2009) argue that just like what colonialism did, a Eurocentric attitude to knowledge has conveniently threatened indigenous knowledge in many [African] societies. Yet, if we are to consider the failure of many scholars including the renowned Leibniz, Popper, Carnpa and Lakatos, to find satisfactory demarcation criteria between science and non-science, we would be correct to argue that it is indeed unnecessary to draw solid lines between Western (modern) and Indigenous knowledge (see also Bhola 2002). Each knowledge form – whether Western science or African science (the so-called indigenous knowledge) – should be treated as distinct, valid and important in its own terms, and should be evaluated by its own criterion. For this reason, there is urgent need for Africa to come to the drawing board and come up with a clear and 'official' framework or plan of action on what should be done for the continent to build on all the valuable indigenous capitals of its historical past, drop out all that is counterproductive and detrimental to her development and sustainability. This is critical to guarantee Africa's freedom and ability to determine its own destination. In fact, I agree with Asante (cited in Mengara 2001: xv) that the negative "images of Africa will not remain forever locked in the negative chambers of the past…[but] an Africa that is freed of the imposition of others and consequently an Africa that could rise at any occasion"; hence the need to brain storm on what possibly could be done for Africa's indigenous knowledge in order for the continent to come out of the quagmire that it was dragged and trapped into throughout the course of its colonial history.

What should the development community do about IK?

The value of indigenous knowledge cannot be underestimated any longer. Talking of the value of 'traditional' or indigenous medicines, for example, Bodeker and Kronenberg (2002) reveal that apart from modern pharmaceutical usage, traditional systems of medicine and alternative and complementary medicine represent up to 50% of use in many industrialised countries and up to 80% in many developing nations. In fact, it is now generally agreed by both scholars and development experts that indigenous knowledge is indispensable for [community] development especially in former colonised societies. There is need, therefore, for an urgent plan of action or framework on how development community could make use of indigenous knowledge in their projects in Africa and beyond. The World Bank (1998: ii-iii) proposes a framework for action for development community revolving around four pillars explicated below:

a). Disseminating information:

♦Developing a database of IK practices, lessons learned, sources, partners, etc.

♦Identifying and testing instruments for capture and dissemination of IK.

♦Publishing selected cases in print and electronic format.

b). Facilitating exchange of IK among developing country communities:

♦Helping build local capacity to share IK, especially among the local IK centres.

♦Identifying appropriate methods of capturing, disseminating IK among communities.

♦Facilitating a global network to exchange IK.

c). Applying indigenous knowledge in the development process:

♦Raising awareness of the importance of IK among development partners.

♦Helping countries to prepare national policies in support of indigenous practices.

♦Integrating indigenous practices in programs/projects supported by partners.

d). Building partnerships:

♦Learning from local communities and NGOs.

♦Leveraging limited resources of partners to obtain greater impact on the ground.

♦Addressing the intellectual property rights issue of indigenous knowledge.

Making use of the proposed framework, the World Bank and the partnership that has developed around the indigenous knowledge initiative (namely Centre for International Research and Advisory Networks (CIRAN) at Nuffic, Centre for Information Society Development in Africa (CISDA), UN Economic Commission for Africa (ECA), International Development Research Centre of Canada (IDRC), UN International Telecommunications Union (ITU), Southern Africa NGO Internet Provider (SANGO Net), UN Development Programme (UNDP), UN Educational, Scientific and Cultural Organisation (UNESCO), UN World Health Organisation (WHO), World Intellectual Property

Organisation (WIPO) and World Bank [lead partner]) (see World Bank 1998: 1) elaborated an initial plan of action for the period 1998-99, which included specific objectives and deliverables. As dictated by the framework, each of the aforementioned partner institution was required to undertake activities consistent with the respective institutional policies as well as procedures. To provide input on strategic planning, implementation and monitoring of the activities, an external advisory panel composed of representatives of partner institutions was established. The initial main focus of the partner activities were considered to be three-fold: increase awareness of IK; disseminate IK practices; and help build the capacity of local indigenous knowledge centres to further identify, document and disseminate IK practices (World Bank 1998: iii). To kick start the initiative, it was agreed that partners provide financial support to local indigenous knowledge centres for researches around indigenous knowledge and related practices. On the same stroke, the partner institutions were also tasked to establish internet connectivity between indigenous knowledge local centres to facilitate the exchange of indigenous knowledge practices and related information across communities. Since development partners were anticipated to encounter challenges on how to integrate indigenous knowledge practices in the development project planning and implementation phases, the World Bank (Ibid) suggested the following in dealing with the challenges:

> *Awareness raising among those who offer development advice; listening to and hearing clients to learn from local communities about what they know; and combining local knowledge with experience from around the world to find relevant and realistic solutions to the development problems of local communities.*

Yet even though the World Bank (1998) has drawn the abovementioned framework for IKs for development, some scholars like Meki Nzewi (2007) remain suspicious of the role of development community especially that the community [development] is masterminded, implemented and monitored by the Euro-American based institutions (like World Bank, among others) instead of those in formerly colonised societies. In fact Nzewi (2007: 4)—strongly feels that "contemporary Africans must strive to rescue, resuscitate and advance our original intellectual legacy, or else the onslaught of externally manipulated forces of mental and cultural dissociation now rampaging Africa will obliterate our original intellect and lore of life. While I agree with Nzewi to a greater extent, in this book, I go beyond Nzewi to advance the World Bank framework and underline that given the sad colonial history that Africa has experienced, there is need for integrated knowledge. Instead of "developing an ecologically coded African society which excludes the traditions of knowing of other peoples, an inclusive system and process of traditional knowledge should be deliberately and vigorously sought and implemented in the education system of the countries" (Maila and Loubser 2003: 278) that were formerly colonised. As Maila and Loubser (2003: 278) further argue, "such an approach will not only be enriching, but will ensure that mistakes of the past are never repeated in regard to elevating a particular knowledge system above another". This is similar to what Mignolo (2000) and Grosfoguel (2006) refer to as critical border thinking – a concept with which they critique both imperial fundamentalism and fundamentalism of the subaltern. Also, with diverse problems – social, economic, environmental, political and others – becoming more diverse and complex with the passage of time, continents should work closely in utilising and develop other systems of knowledge (whether indigenous, modern, Eastern, Western or African) that help the world in dealing with pressing problems across the board (see also Maila 2001; Maila and Loubser 2003). Ngugi wa Thiongo (1986) concurs with this thinking as he sees the fruition of this possibility only if the liberation of natural and human resources and the entire production forces of the nation, would be considered the beginning of Africa's real socio-economic and political progress and development. Semali and Kincheloe (1999: 37-38) also concurs when they argue:

> *A curriculum that values subjugated knowledge in general realises that indigenous knowledge is important not only for the culture that produced it but for the people from different cultures. Only now at the end of the twentieth century are European peoples beginning to appreciate the value of indigenous knowledge about health, medicine, agriculture, philosophy, ecology, and education.*

Wa Thiongo, Semali and Kincheloe, thus, advocate an integrated curriculum that does not privilege particular forms of knowledge but recognises the value of all forms of knowledge including indigenous knowledge.

Chapter 3

Indigenous Knowledge and Adaptation: Some Showcases from Africa

Any human society (be it African, European, Indian etc.) has knowledge that is indigenous to its own people. Africa, thus, is not an exception to this truism, and it is a well-known fact that Africa as a continent is richly endowed with varied indigenous practices, technologies, and knowledge systems. Some of its practices, technologies and knowledge systems have been studied extensively by ethnologists, social anthropologists, and sector specialists (see for example Mwadime 1999; Semali and Kincheloe 1999). The major problem with most of these studies, however, is that they tend to be largely descriptive and theoretical. The World Bank (1998: 2) captures this observation aptly when it notes that the problem with most of the studies around IKs is that:

> *They concentrate primarily on the social or ethnological aspects of knowledge rather than on the technical ones. The literature contains limited information regarding the systematic transfer of local knowledge across communities and cultures. Yet, there is considerable impressionistic evidence of IK transfer from traditional societies to industrial countries (e.g., acupuncture, herbal medicine, rehydration salts, etc.).*

In view of this critical observation, this chapter is devoted to showcase indigenous knowledges from the continent of Africa. The chapter goes beyond documenting IKs in areas such as agriculture, health care, technology, and poverty alleviation, among others by emphasising the non-stasis and transferability of the IKs from one community to another. In the section below, I discuss how IKs can be successfully transferred and exchanged between communities whether African or otherwise.

Indigenous knowledge exchange: Some steps to IK exchange

To achieve development in rural and even in urban communities, it is not only possible but beneficial to exchange IKs between communities so that the communities could enrich the other. But for this to happen, and in order to integrate IKs into the development process of communities, a process of exchange of information between communities in developing countries and between developing and industrialised countries is important. Towards this realisation, World Bank (1998: ii) suggests six important steps to be followed:

◆*Recognition and identification*
Some IKs may be embedded in a mix of technologies or in cultural values, rendering them unrecognisable at first glance to the external observer (technical and social analyses may, therefore, be required to identify IK);

◆*Validation*
This involves an assessment of IK's significance and relevance (to solving problems), reliability (i.e., not being an accidental occurrence), functionality (how well does it work?), effectiveness and transferability;

♦Recording and documentation

Recording and documentation is a major challenge because of the tacit nature of IK (it is typically exchanged through personal communication from master to apprentice, from parent to child, etc.). In some cases, modern tools could be used, while in other circumstances it may be appropriate to rely on more traditional methods (e.g., taped narration, drawings);

♦Storage in retrievable repositories

Storage is not limited to text document or electronic format; it could include tapes, films, story-telling, gene banks, etc.

♦Transfer

This step goes beyond merely conveying the knowledge to the recipient; it also includes the testing of the knowledge in the new environment. Pilots are the most appropriate approach in this step; and

♦Dissemination

Dissemination to a wider community adds the developmental dimension to the exchange of knowledge and could promote a wider and deeper ripple impact of the knowledge transfer.

Transfer and application of indigenous knowledge: Some critical case studies

Investing in the application, exchange, and transfer of indigenous knowledge and its integration into the assistance programmes of the World Bank and its development partners such as non-governmental organisations (NGOs) or such other development agencies can help to reduce or even eradicate poverty in Africa and beyond. By indigenous knowledge transfer, I mean the process whereby any indigenous knowledge is disseminated or transmitted from its area of origin to be used (application) in another area. I should emphasise that this is a learning process to both the agent who transmit the indigenous knowledge/practice and the community that receives (recipient), adopts and adapts the practice. There are many cases, documented and undocumented, of indigenous knowledges that have been transmitted (and can still be shared, exchanged or transmitted) from one community to another: case studies that were selected to correct the thinking of some scholars that indigenous knowledge is static and immovable. Below are some of the selected few examples of such IKs found across the African continent:

Case One

Application: *Zimbabwe and western Mozambique – Traditional rules and spiritual controls in conservation to protect land, natural forests, non-timber forest products and regulate their use.*

In many African societies such as Zimbabwe and Mozambique, there are traditional customs, values, and religious belief systems that help communities with environmental conservation mechanisms that ensure sustainability. To this effect, there are *madambakurimwa* (singular: *dambakurimwa*, literally known as places that resist cultivation), which are vast ecological reserves for natural growth and activity. These woodlands whose boundaries, manner of conduct when within them [the areas], and rules are normally defined by traditional leadership [chiefs and headmen] and spirit mediums of a given area, are sacred such that tree cutting, cultivation, uncontrolled firewood collection, hunting, fruit harvesting, and livestock grazing are prohibited. Human disturbance of the natural processes and activities that take place in these areas is, therefore, restricted such that even fruits are normally prohibited from carrying home or harvesting for sale: they should be harvested and eaten on site. When in these areas, pronouncement of obscene things or commending on objects, structures, or anything that belongs to the *madambakurimwa* is even prohibited. Those who violate the rules are believed to be punished by misfortune and sometimes death by the ancestral spirits of the land. Some of the common punishments in these areas include being attacked by *mhondoro* (ancestral lions) or some wild animals, *chadzimira* (literally mean getting lost in the *dambakurimwa*), and being stung by mysterious bees.

Lesson learnt: Conservation in ecological zones protected through traditional rules and spiritual controls is far much better in terms of yielding results if it is to be compared with National Parks/game reserves where administration is executed through statutory law and bureaucratic procedures. Besides, such conservation is cost effective as unlike in National Parks/game reserves where employees are paid monthly for their services, traditional leadership and spirit mediums who take part in the conservation are not.**(Source:** *Personal communication*).

Case Two

Application: *Mozambique – Transfer of tototo beer brewing system (using traditional distillation apparatus/process) from western and central to southern provinces.*

For many years now, a traditionally brewed beer known as *tototo* has been brewed in the western and central provinces of Mozambique. *Tototo* beer, which is brewed through the distillation of ripen fruits such as mangoes, bananas, oranges, or sugarcane, is estimated to be five times stronger than commercially brewed beer such as black label, montelo, castle larger and others. *Tototo* beer brewing system of the Manica province of Mozambique which is believed to have developed three or four centuries ago was transferred to Inhambane and Xai-Xai provinces of southern Mozambique when Ngungunyane migrated from Manica province to settle in the Manjacaze district of Xai-Xai province after being defeated by the Portuguese. To date, *tototo* is brewed in both the western and central provinces of Mozambique (where it originated) and in the southern provinces of the country where the system was transferred to. The beer is normally brewed by women and is used for recreational purposes.

Lesson learnt: Such activities as *tototo* beer brewing help us to understand the central role played by women in society, particularly when it comes to issues to do with recreation and family sustenance. As a source of additional income, *tototo* brewing can be useful to local communities and in raising the socio-economic status of women when there is a seasonal surplus of fruits such as mangoes, oranges, bananas and also sugarcane. (**Source:** *Personal communication*).

48

Case Three

Application: *Tanzania – Producing Enaisho Olotorok wine from honey for cultural and ritual purposes is an important activity for women in Maasai society.*

Enaisho Olotorok (a local brew made wine of bee honey) is of great symbolic importance to the Maasai of Tanzania. It is directly related to those rituals and ceremonies that are held most sacred. *Enaisho Olotorok* is made only for ceremonial purposes and is not sold commercially or brewed to drink recreationally. It is brewed for the most significant ceremonies in Maasai culture, such as psycho-somatic prayers, circumcision, marriage and age-set promotion. Women are the specialists to perform the brewing process. The importance of the rituals and ceremonies for which *Enaisho Olotorok* is produced indicates the importance of the role of women in the community.

Lesson learnt: This activity helps us understanding that the role of women in Maasai ceremonies is central to understand their role in Maasai society. **(Source:** *Masailand Resource Centre for Indigenous Knowledge (MARECIK)).*

Case Four

Application: *Zimbabwe—Introducing biological organisms instead of chemicals as method to control house flies and mosquitoes.*

Zimbabwe receives most of its rainfall in summer, and February is known as the breeding month for flies. This breeding month for house flies coincides with the time when green meali-cobs and other crops are harvested for consumption from the fields: there are many flies during this time. During this period, people in southern Zimbabwe collect spiders in small [spider] webs from the forest and introduce them around the cupboards and dark corners in the kitchen. The spider webs trap any housefly, cockroach, mosquito and other [kitchen] small insects that come into contact with them [webs]. The trapped insects are eaten by the spiders. This way, people reduce the problem of house flies, cockroaches, and mosquitoes which are indeed nuisances and also cause/transmit diseases to human beings. The activity is normally carried out by women and children.

Lesson learnt: This shows that cost effective methods of controlling house flies that are local and health can be more advantageous as compared to the use of chemicals such as DDT that are both expensive and with side effects to human health. This activity also shows the central role that women and children play in society, particularly in helping controlling the spreading of diseases.(**Source:** *Personal communication*).

Case Five

Application: *Tanzania and Rwanda – Transfer of the Washambaa Agricultural System of Tanzania to Rwanda, adaptation, and re-transfer.*

The Washambaa of the Usambara Mountains in Tanzania had developed a land use system emulating the climax vegetation of the deciduous natural forest. They integrated annuals and perennials on the same plot in a multi-story arrangement. The principles were transferred to Nyabisindu, Rwanda in a German Development Cooperation (GTZ) assisted project; and special multi-purpose contour bunds with trees shrubs and fodder grasses were added to the system. The adapted practice was later re-transferred to the Washambaa once dense population and need for firewood had depleted the soil cover and demand for dairy products had initiated the introduction of improved cattle breeds.

Lesson learnt: This shows that emulation of natural vegetation is a valid approach to soil conservation; and also that transferring and adding elements to address new problems adds value to the original concepts and indigenous knowledges, leading to effective exchange of knowledge. (**Source:** *World Bank, 1998/99 World Development Report*).

Case Six

Application: *Zimbabwe – Use of Pfimbi System to preserve sweet potatoes after harvesting.*

In Zimbabwe, sweet potato is one of the tubers grown towards the end of rain season (normally in February). They are used for breakfast in the morning as they are normally taken together with tea or coffee. In preserving sweet potatoes that they stay longer than they naturally do, people in Zimbabwe use *pfimbi* (literally known as sweet potato pits) system. Pits of about 50cm to 1m (depending on the amount of sweet potatoes to be preserved) are dug. Sweet potatoes are then put in the pit before the mouth of the pit is sealed or closed using a lid. When needed, the lead is removed and re-sealed/closed. This is an efficient system for preserving sweet potatoes. Using this method, the sweet potatoes can be preserved for up to six months, that is, up to the onset of the subsequent rain season.

Lesson learnt: This shows that simple, locally developed knowledges and technologies adapted to their environment, are affordable for local communities, and may contribute to improving their lives. Food stuffs that can stay only for a few days, thus, can be preserved for longer periods using traditional means that are cost effective. (**Source:** *Personal communication*).

Case Seven

Application: *Tanzania – Biotic weather forecasting (based on ecology and meteorology).*

The Maasai people of Tanzania alternate the use of their natural grassland according to seasons. This requires a timely decision on when and where to move next based on their knowledge of seasons. Besides, the Maasai people predict droughts as well as weather related diseases by watching the movements of celestial bodies in combination with observing the date of emergence of certain plant species (e.g. *Ole Kitolya*). Such "early warning signals" of an approaching environmental disaster are used to determine any preventive measures, prepare for mitigation and decide on the course of action of the community in using the natural resources. Similarly, estimates of animal fertility can be drawn from such forecasts with implication on stocking rates and density. This knowledge is little researched so far though its utility among the Maasai people has been proven over the years.

Lesson learnt: This is clear testimony that traditional expertise in astronomy and weather forecasting in combination with conventional agricultural meteorology could enhance local forecasts on harvests and food security. **(Source:** *Masailand Resource Centre for Indigenous Knowledge (MARECIK)).*

Case Eight

Application: *Rwanda – Adoption of modern bean varieties in Columbia and Rwanda.*

Two or three varieties of beans considered by the expert scientists to have the most potential had achieved only modest yield increases. Scientists then invited the women farmers who possessed valuable indigenous knowledge about bean cultivation to examine more than 20 bean varieties at the research stations and to take home and grow the two or three [varieties] they thought most promising. The women farmers planted the new varieties using their own methods of experimentation. Their selections outperformed those of the expert scientists by 60 to 90 percent.

Lesson learnt: This shows that indigenous knowledge can help inform the process of adaptation of modern cultivation techniques. (**Source:** World Bank, *World Development Report*, 1998: 4).

Case Nine

Application: *Tanzania – Maasai pastoralists' veterinary practices for the prevention and treatment of diseases in livestock.*

The Maasai pastoralists of Tanzania have developed their own strategies to prevent and treat contagious livestock diseases such as rinderpest, contagious bovine pleuro-pneumonia (CBPP), anthrax / black leg, foot and mouth disease, brucellosis, among many others. Medicinal plants and plant preparations are used as disinfectants, anaesthetics, styptics, anti-inflammatory, pyretics, and appetisers and as anti-microbial agents. Routing of herds and separation of sick animals are other elements of such strategies, based on early indications of diseases. Surgical techniques include dislocation correction, compound fracture bone setting, castration, obstetrical operations, dental correction, opening (and closing) of artery orifices, removing defected eyes, etc.

Lesson learnt: This shows that traditional veterinary practices provide a low cost approach to livestock hygiene and maintenance of healthy stock. **(Source:** *Masailand Resource Centre for Indigenous Knowledge (MARECIK))*.

Case Ten

Application: *Zimbabwe –The use of ivhu rechuru (termite mound/anthill soil) as natural fertiliser to increase soil fertility in gardens and farmlands.*

In Zimbabwe, small-scale farmers have, since time immemorial, been using *ivhu rechuru* (literally known as anthill soil) to fertilise or improve their agricultural land. The soil from termite mound/anthill soil is dug and then spread evenly in the agricultural land (field or garden). The farmers will then plough using ox-drawn ploughs thereby mixing the anthill soil with the soil in the field. It is confirmed by [expert] scientists that *majuru* (white ants) recover (from deeper soil layers) soil nutrients that will have leached or washed down during raining. For this reason, among others, white ants are regarded as beneficial insects and protected as they provide farmers with cheap natural fertiliser to improve their agricultural land. When digging the termite mounds, farmers make sure that the mounds are not totally destroyed so that the termites will continue building the mounds thereby ensuring farmers that they can continue to rely on them once again after some years of recovery. The productivity of land that has been fed with anthill soil is reported as having increased considerably, much better than artificial fertilisers (such as ammonium nitrate) whose effect normally lasts for a season.

Lesson learnt: This shows that instead of relying on artificially made fertilisers that are in most cases expensive and short-lived, farmers can rely on cost effective means to fertilise their agricultural land and still improve their crop yields. Also in times of economic difficulties, farmers could overcome financial constraints for their agricultural activities by relying on local resources such as termite mounds. **(Source:** *Personal communication*).

Case Eleven

Application: *Cameroon – Long term storage of cassava.*

The Balong people of Cameroon have a traditional technology of processing cassava (*Manihot esculenta*) into a product called *Kumkum* that can be preserved for up to five years. Freshly harvested roots are peeled, washed and steeped in water and left to stand for three to five days during which natural fermentation takes place and the tuberous roots are softened. They are removed and ground into a fine paste, then placed in a cane basket and covered with plantain leaves. Heavy objects such as stones are piled on the pulp to drain off excess liquor. Some 200-300 grams are hand – moulded into round balls and placed on a platform which is hung over the hearth to dry out gradually. Due to constant fire at the site, the balls gradually are coated with smoke. During the storage period, which varies from one to five years, the product is hardly ever attacked by pests or disease. When needed, the black coating on the balls is scraped off. They are then re-pounded into fine flour, which is reconstituted with hot water into dough, and eaten with soup or vegetable stew.

Lesson learnt: Traditional methods of storage can be explored for disaster preparedness. Such traditional methods of storage are also cost effective as compared to commercially made chemicals for pest control during storage. **(Source:** *Cameroon Indigenous Knowledge Organisation (CIKO))*.

Case Twelve

Application: *Nigeria – Use of natural refrigeration system.*

An inventor from northern Nigeria (Jigawa State) has developed an efficient electricity-free, "pot-in-pot" cooling system that is affordable for local communities, and now widely used by them. The system consists of two different-sized earthenware pots, one inside the other. The space between them is filled with water-retentive sand. Perishable food such as eggplants, okra and tomatoes, is placed in the smaller pot and covered with a cloth. The pots are placed in a dry, ventilated spot and the sand is periodically watered. As the water in the sand evaporates into the drier air outside, it cools the pots and their contents. Keeping eggplants fresh for a month, instead of three days, and tomatoes and pepper for more than three weeks, has helped farmers avoid having to sell their produce immediately, and has reduced diseases caused by rotting food. This has resulted in an increase in farmers' incomes, slowing the movement of population from country to city in northern Nigeria. The inventor estimates the use of this natural refrigeration system at three-quarters of the rural families in Jigawa State. In addition, women are considered the biggest beneficiaries of this invention. Indeed, it is reported that women selling fruits and vegetables from their homes could earn an income, and girls who were sent to sell food before it spoiled can now go to school.

Lesson learnt: This shows that simple, locally developed technologies adapted to their environment, are affordable for local communities, and may contribute to improving their lives. **(Source:** *Financial Times, Monday October 9, 2000: (Adopted from the article: 'Staying cool naturally', by Carola Hoyos*).

Case Thirteen

Application: *Cameroon – Use of sorghum stalks as a source of salt.*

Northern Cameroon is a leading cattle producing region, where salt is in very high demand. In 1994, after the devaluation of the *cfa franc*, the price of salt increased by 400%, and since then its supply has been fluctuating, causing periodic price hikes. To cope with this situation, the

Moundang and Toupouri people who live in the Mayo-Kebbi District in the Northern Province of Cameroon have developed a technology to make salt from dry stalks of sorghum plants. Prior to this, sorghum stalks did not serve any useful purpose. In this case, the stalks are gathered and burned, and the remaining ash is sieved and boiled in water until it becomes whitish. After cooling, the liquid is left to coagulate. At that stage, it is ready for consumption as a substitute for salt. Only two other inputs, namely, fire and water, are needed for the processing. This kind of salt, called "garlaka", is produced by women who are said to earn up to 250.000 *cfa francs* per year in selling it.

Lesson learnt: Knowing the various uses of underutilised plants may allow people to cope with resource shortages and can help generate income for rural communities. **(Source:** *Cameroon Indigenous Knowledge Organisation (CIKO)*).

Case Fourteen

Application: *Mozambique and Zimbabwe – Use of Rukwa to safeguard/protect property from theft.*

In some parts of Mozambique (especially in the central and the west province) and Zimbabwe (esp. in the southern and eastern parts of the country), some people use *rukwa* (literally known as guarding property using magic charm/anti-theft charm) (see Mawere 2011). *Rukwa* is normally used to safeguard field crops and domestic property such as livestock, kitchen utensils, and farm implements from thieves. It is also used by fishers and hunters to protect their catch. In the case of the latter, for example, when a hunter goes into the forest to set a *musungo* (animal trap) for guinea fowls, rabbits or other animals, one should never dare stealing from the trap. It is commonly known that wild game belongs to everyone in the community but once the animal is in the trap, it now belongs to the hunter. If one steals from hunters who use *rukwa* to protect their catch from thieves, the thief will be caught by the *rukwa*. The thief will not be able to go away with the stolen animal until the owner of the animal comes to set him/her free. If the owner takes too long (say several days) before coming to check his trap, the thief may die from hunger. This is a very effective way for safeguarding property that deters potential thieves as it does not only attract fines, but also embarrassment on the part of the thief.

Lesson learnt: This shows that traditional mechanisms used to safeguard/protect property from thieves are even more efficient and cost effective than those normally used commercially such as employing security guards. Such a mechanism as *rukwa*, for example, can be used in banks, supermarkets and other business premises to reduce the economic burden of employing dozens of security workers. One *rukwa*, for example, can perform work that several people would do in business premises. It can also be sold to property owners thereby enhancing the economic status of the rural people or communities who own the *rukwa*. (**Source:** *Mawere 2011*).

Case Fifteen

Application: *Cameroon-Ethno-veterinary practices.*

In the North-western province of Cameroon, ethno-veterinarians and experts from the Ministries responsible for Livestock, Fisheries and Animal Industries, and the Institute for Animal Research joined forces in cooperation with Heifer Project International (HPI) to deal with veterinary drugs and services problems. The Ethno-veterinary Medicine/Fulani Livestock Development Project, thus, addresses the problem of expensive and erratic supply of veterinary drugs and services to seek a sustainable way of improving animal health in the region by a complementary utilisation of indigenous and orthodox veterinary medicines. Benefits are a reduction of dependency on imported veterinary drugs and supplies, the possibility of discovering new drugs and the use of natural drugs with fewer side effects. The communication and contacts between livestock owners and veterinarians have improved; Cameroon's first association of traditional veterinarians was founded and active networking among indigenous practitioners and orthodox animal health care specialists was promoted. Some traditional herbal treatments, taxonomy of active plants and food and dairy processing practices were documented.

Lesson learnt: Building on indigenous knowledge not only assists in the achievement of technical objectives but improves communication between beneficiaries, traditional and modern experts and the exchange and transfer of knowledge. (**Source:** *Cameroon Indigenous Knowledge Organisation (CIKO)*).

Case Sixteen

Application: *Mozambique and Zimbabwe – Sun drying of vegetables, edible insects, mushroom, and fruits.*

In Mozambique and Zimbabwe, green vegetables, tomatoes, edible insects, some fruits are sun dried to preserve them so that they stay for longer period before they go bad. Here, usually two ways/methods of sun drying are practised. One method used to preserve the aforementioned foodstuffs, for example, vegetables is immersion. Immersion is whereby fresh vegetables are cut into small pieces before they are immersed/ dipped in salty boiling water for a few minutes to avoid nutrient loss. The vegetables are then spread evenly on a sack or tier and left to dry in the sun for about two to three days (depending on weather). The dried vegetables (locally named *mufushwa* or *musoni* in Zimbabwe and central-western Mozambique) are stored in a safe dry place and can last for two to four years. The same method is also applied for drying edible stinkbugs, mushroom, Mopani worms, termites, white ants and other edible insects. The second method is to directly spread the cut fresh vegetables, collected fruits or edible insects in the sun. Depending on how long the food is needed to preserve, it can either be salted (if needed to preserve for a longer period) or not (if needed to preserve for a shorter period). In Mozambique and Zimbabwe, sun drying of food is normally done by women as they culturally bear the responsibility for food preparation for their respective families.

Lesson learnt: This activity helps us to understand the central role played by women in society, particularly when it comes to issues to do with food preparation and preservation. Also, the activity shows that sun drying is an affordable technology requiring little or no intervention under most conditions in the tropical countries such as Zimbabwe and Mozambique where sunshine is abundant. Besides, such local methods for preserving food stuffs can help to enhance the economic status of women as the food stuffs can be taken for marketing in townships and urban areas. **(Source:** *Personal communication*).

Case Seventeen

Application: *Cameroon – The use of organic fertilizer.*

Foulbe farmers from Garoua in the North Province of Cameroon have been emulating a soil fertilisation technique, which originated in the neighbouring Republic of Chad. They use cattle horns for soil fertilisation in fruit tree orchards and farms. A set of two horns from freshly slaughtered cattle are placed on the ground at distances ranging 40 to 75 centimetres from the tree. The horns attract certain insects which, while feeding on them, fertilise the soil with their secretions. Yields in farms and orchards, where this technology has been applied, have increased by 75%, as confirmed by the Agronomy Research Station of Garoua.

Lesson learnt: Agricultural extension should promote the use of certain organic manure, developed and produced by local communities, and successfully transferred from one country to another. (**Source:** *Cameroon Indigenous Knowledge Organisation (CIKO)*).

Case Eighteen

Application: *Mozambique and Zimbabwe – Mixed cropping techniques.*

In southern Zimbabwe and most other areas in Mozambique with limited precipitation, farmers seek optimal crop yield by growing both long and short growth cycle crops such as millet, watermelon, and sorghum on the same plot. This agricultural practice allows farmers to spread risk over a large number of varieties and, therefore, increasing possibilities for success. For instance, millet seeds of various cycles are mixed and sowed in the same plot such that harvesting is performed during the staggered ripening period. Mixed cropping techniques thus allow farmers to insure a certain food security and reduce drought risks linked to erratic or unpredictable rainfall.

Lesson learnt: The agricultural techniques elaborated above mean that risk reduction strategy, while useful to ensure household food security, is incompatible with the planting of most commercial seeds and should be carefully re-assessed prior to introducing new varieties normally used by commercial farmers. Unlike in commercial farming, the risk reduction strategy used by small-scale farmers is useful to ensure household food security. This risk reduction strategy is incompatible with the planting of most commercial seeds where pesticides and herbicides are normally used. **(Source:** *Personal communication*).

Case Nineteen

Application: *Mozambique – Farmers supply a variety of ridging techniques such as ngare or mhindu ridges.*

In western and northern Mozambique, some farmers use *ngare* or *mhindu* ridges to control erosion and conserve moisture in their fields. *Ngare* ridging is a technique of forming a continuous lump of elevated earth mount during cultivation. Seeds are sown on top and other crops are broadcast at random in a mixed fashion. The ridges check erosion and conserve water. *Ngare* ridges are built across the field to reduce the speed of rainwater and run-off. At the same time they do not amass the water with the danger of breaking the ridges. They channel excess water into grass-covered edges of the field. Studies have shown that *ngare* or *mhindu* ridging are superior to contour ridges on steep slopes. Another type of ridging is the *miwundo* raised bed. Raised beds are especially made for sweet potatoes to drain out excess water in wetlands cultivation. Ridging has proved to be very effective in maintaining the required water balance needed for different varieties of crops even under mixed cultivation. The plants requiring more water are grown in the lower strips where water is abundant, whereas those that need less water are grown on top of the ridge which is well drained.

Lesson learnt: Scientists in the country and from abroad have learned from these techniques, develop them further, e.g. into "tied ridges" and disseminated them to other regions in Africa and beyond. **(Source:** *Zimbabwe Resource Centre for Indigenous Knowledge (ZIRCIK). Also captured by Sadomba 1999).*

Case Twenty

Application: *Ethiopia – Gebeto used as fertilisers for farmlands.*

Farmers in Northern Ethiopia, especially in the Agaw Mider region, use a seed called *gebeto* as a fertiliser. The seed which looks like a bean (with a very sour taste that is not appreciated by birds) is sown in the fields some six months before sowing time for maize, wheat and other cereals. The plant that grows is not harvested but left to dry, and becomes a natural fertiliser. The farmers would then plough their fields and sow cereals. With this soil fertilisation method, production is reported to increase substantially. Another use of *gebeto* is for medical purposes. A handful of this bean cooked and taken orally every morning is used to reduce blood pressure, by the people of Northern Ethiopia.

Lesson learnt: This shows that traditional methods of soil fertilisation are cost effective, hence worth preserving and promoting for rural community development. **(Source:** *Association for the Promotion of Indigenous Knowledge (APIK)).*

Case Twenty-One

Application: *Zimbabwe and Mozambique – Use of Runyoka to deal with the problems of infidelity and HIV/Aids.*

Infidelity and HIV/Aids are common problems in many societies across the world. In some parts of Zimbabwe (eastern and northern) and Mozambique (northern, central and western parts), some people use *runyoka/muzazata* (literally known as fencing a wife/husband using charm) to control sexual behaviours of their own spouses, promote fidelity, and also to reduce the risks of contracting the deadly disease, HIV/Aids (see also Mawere 2011). *Runyoka* can be used by either a wife to his husband or vice versa, but normally without the knowledge of the other. Sometimes it is also used by parents as a mechanism to promote good moral sexual behaviour in their children especially young girls. Anyone who sleeps around with a woman or man who has been fenced by *runyoka* will face serious consequences. The consequences vary. Sometimes the pair will not be able to separate from each other once they have a sexual encounter until the one who set the *runyoka* comes to their rescue. If assistance in this instance is delayed, the end result for the pair will be death. This is a very efficient and cost effective mechanism of controlling human behaviour and also the spreading of HIV/Aids.

Lesson learnt: This system shows that if some traditional mechanisms are adopted to deal with problems of infidelity and sexually transmitted diseases such as HIV/Aids, they are even more efficient than those being used in the mainstream medical fraternity. If sold to other communities, this can also generate revenue for the owners/manufactures of *runyoka* thereby enhancing their socio-economic status. (**Source:** *Mawere 2011*).

Case Twenty-Two

Application: *Burkina Faso – Mossi soil conservation practices.*

In Burkina Faso, small-scale farmers use mossi conservation practices to protect their fields from erosion and to maintain high fertility levels in the soil. Mossi soil conservation practices include the application of farmyard manure, strip fallow, rotational fallow, building of micro-catchments, mulching and reforestation. These ecologically sound methods are particularly valuable when combined with building stone contour bunds for alleviating an imbalance in soil fertility.

Lesson learnt: This means that agricultural extension services needs to build on these techniques when introducing new technologies or varieties as a way of enhancing farmers' agricultural knowledge. This would empower instead of disempower local farmers thereby putting them in a better position to fight poverty and develop their own communities through agriculture. (**Source:** *Jean Yves Marchal 1986*).

Case Twenty-Three

Application: *Zimbabwe – Use of Zumbani (Lippia javanica) to control chicken flea.*

Chicken flea is a common parasite for poultry keepers in Zimbabwe. To deal with the parasite, some people across the country use leaves of a plant that grows naturally in the forest known locally as *zumbani (Lippia javanica). Zumbani* leaves have chemicals that kill chicken flea in just a few days' time. When there is an outbreak of chicken flea, people collect *zumbani* green leaves from the forest and hang them in the fowl run or around the chicken nests (in the case of laying hens). In just a few days' time, the chicken flea will have been eradicated.

Lesson learnt: This shows that scientists and poultry keepers across the world can learn from traditional techniques and develop them where necessary. This also shows that some traditional methods of controlling poultry diseases are cost effective as compared to industrially manufactured chemicals. (**Source:** *Personal communication*).

Case Twenty-Four

Application: *Zambia – Sustainable wildlife management.*

In Zambia, both the Barotse people and the Bemba of Luapula province had (and still have in many in parts of the province) a tradition of avoiding the catching of very small fish. Communities observed fishing seasons usually through a set of traditional ceremonies. Such a ceremony would usually open the fishing season for a given period. These practices ensured that sustainable resource exploitation.

Lesson learnt: This means that state wildlife agents and external development should consider management epistemologies and build on them if they want to promote sustainability and development in rural communities. (**Source:** *World Bank, 2004: 31*).

Case Twenty-Five

Application: *Zimbabwe and Mozambique – Taboos restrict extractive use of medicinal plant species and for water management.*

More often than not, development agents and scholars that are Western biased dismiss beliefs, especially those associated with social behaviour and taboos (locally named *zviera* in Zimbabwe and western Mozambique) as superstitions and unscientific. For these reasons the intrinsic values and functions of taboos are often despised and their use underestimated. What these scientists do not understand is that in many cases, the superstitions (taboos) are not meant to convey 'scientific' facts but to shape thinking, and to control human behaviour. Taboos are social rules engrained in people of a particular area through the process of socialisation (see also Gelfand 1979; Tatira 2000; Mawere 2010). Where taboos are used, for example, in the protection of forests, rivers, wells, and grave yards, fear normally develops in all those who value the taboos such that they believe violation of the taboos result in infliction of punishment by ancestors and sometimes traditional leadership. Taboos used in protecting forests have the function of preserving medicinal plant species and fruit tree species. In the case of medicinal plant species, for example, there is a common belief by herbalists and traditional healers that when extracting the bark of a tree for use as medicine, one should only remove barks from the sides facing the east and west of the tree. Extracting the barks from all sides, including the south and north of the tree is believed to be ineffective because one will have broken the taboo. By following this taboo, trees easily survive the extraction; hence medicinal plant species are managed sustainably.

Lesson learnt: The important lesson from this activity is that communities could consider developing new taboos for the management of natural resources that have become scarce or that are being threatened to extinction. Also, ownership of water and sanitation programmes may increase if project planner acknowledge and appreciate the already existing customs that work in favour of sustainable use and management of resources. (**Source:** *Gelfand 1979; Tatira 2000; Mawere 2010*).

Case Twenty-Six

Application: *Mozambique and Zimbabwe – Weather forecasting based on ecology and meteorology.*

The Shona and Ndau people of Mozambique and Zimbabwe respectively predict weather as well as drought by watching the movements of animals such as tortoises, and by listening to sounds of birds such as *dendera* (hornbill) and *gunguwo* (crow). In western Mozambique, for example, if people see tortoises moving fast up the hills and mountains they know it is a sign of heavy oncoming rains. In southern Zimbabwe, if people hear the *dendera* bird (plural-*matendera*) singing early in the morning, it is a warning sign that rains are coming soon. Many other birds are also used to predict weather. If the crow caws in the morning after a downpour or a prolonged drizzle, it's a sign that the drizzle is coming to an end. So are the sounds of frogs. When frogs cackle in a dry hot day, it is a warning sign for impending heavy rains. Such warning signals of what may happen in the imminent future are used to determine any preventive measures, prepare for mitigation and decide on the course of action of the community in terms of planning and preparing their daily activities. This knowledge is little researched so far, yet proves to be very efficient and cost effective.

Lesson learnt: This shows that traditional expertise in astronomy and weather forecasting in combination with conventional agricultural meteorology could enhance local forecasts and help farmers to plan their daily activities, harvests and food security. (**Source:** *Personal communication*).

Case Twenty-Seven

Application: *Zimbabwe – Ethno-veterinary practices*

In Zimbabwe, especially among the Shona people, when one is suffering from malaria, people normally use plants like chiparurangoma (*Borreria dibrachiata*) as a form of treatment. Chiparurangoma, which is still used in some places in southern and eastern Zimbabwe, is administered orally and the patient usually heals of the ailment within twenty-four hours or less depending on the type of malaria being cured. Besides chiparurangoma, the Shona people of Zimbabwe also use a kind of shrub locally named muvengahonye (*Canthium huillense*) to treat and heal both human beings and livestock wounds that have become septic. Other plants like *chikohwa/gavakava* (aloe) are used for stomach ailments in people and to treat new castle disease in chicken.

Lesson learnt: This shows that scientists in the medical fraternity and veterinary sciences should seriously consider traditional medicines as a compliment of Western science. This also shows that some traditional methods of controlling poetry and livestock diseases are cost effective as compared to industrially manufactured chemicals that are expensive and sometimes difficult to administer. **(Source:** *Mapara 2009; Also, my personal communication*).

Case Twenty-eight

Application: *Mozambique and Zimbabwe – Traditional dye for domestic mat craft and traditional art.*

In Mozambique and Zimbabwe, dye of different colours is extracted from certain trees such as muchakata (*Parinari curatellifolia*). To extract the dye from muchakata tree, barks of the aforementioned tree are crushed to small pieces. They are then boiled in water for about twenty to thirty minutes depending on the dye concentration required by the artist. After this time, the water will have changed its colour to brown. Artists then use the brown coloured water to decorate their mat crafts and other works of art by sprinkling the water. The dye just like commercially made dye is permanent: once sprinkled on the mats, it won't be removed.

Lesson learnt: This shows that some traditional methods of dyeing mat crafts and decorating traditional art works are more convenient and cost effective as compared to industrially manufactured chemicals. **(Source:** *Personal communication*).

Case Twenty-nine

Application: *Zimbabwe – Medical and veterinary practices.*

Among the Manyika people of Eastern Zimbabwe, a certain plant called *mumwahuku* (*Cassia didymobotrya*) is used to prevent chicken diseases such as *chitosi* (a type of poultry sickness). The mumwahuku plant leaves are collected and pounded in a mortar using a pistil. After pounding, water is added to the medicine before it is given to chicken to drink. The medicine can be taken by chickens that are not yet suffering from the disease as a preventive measure or by chickens that already suffer from the disease as a cure.

Lesson learnt: This is a clear testimony that some traditional medical and veterinary traditional practices are equally effective as Western oriented medical and veterinary practices. Besides, they are more cost effective as compared to Western oriented or industrially manufactured medicines. **(Source:** *Mapara 2009*).

74

Case Thirty

Application: *Zimbabwe – Use of chinjiri to minimise erosion.*

In pre-colonial Zimbabwe, there was utilisation of slopes for cultivation known as *matema* in the Sanyadowa area of Nyanga, eastern Zimbabwe. The use of these areas was stopped by colonial conservation authorities, yet when they cultivated these slopes, the people involved used *chinjiri* (terraces) to minimise the effects of erosion that resulted from run-off water. The colonial authorities did not appreciate these initiatives and ordered them to be stopped instantly. After independence in 1980, the people in eastern highlands resumed the practice of using *chinjiri* which remains an effective measure to minimise steep slope erosion even today.

Lesson learnt: This shows that some traditional methods of soil conservation and environment management are equally or even more effective than the Western biased conservation methods. Besides, they are more cost effective as compared to most of the Western biased environment conservation practices. (**Source:** *Duri and Mapara 2007*).

Case Thirty-one

Application: *Zimbabwe and Mozambique – Use of mujerenjere (Albizia gumifera) as catalyst.*

As early as before the advent of colonialism in Zimbabwe, the Manyika people of Chief Tangwena, Nyanga east in Zimbabwe and the Ndau people of western Mozambique used the leaves of a tree known as *mujerenjere* (*Albizia gumifera*) as a catalyst to hasten the ripening of bananas and paw-paw. In southern Zimbabwe, they use a tree locally known as mufutafuta for the same purpose and also massaging. This indigenous knowledge continues to be used in these areas even today.

Lesson learnt: This shows that some traditional methods of regulating temperatures are equally or even more effective than the Western scientific ones. Besides, they are more cost effective as compared to the Western-biased scientific methods. (**Source**: *Mapara 2009; Also my personal communication*).

Case Thirty-two

Application: *Zimbabwe, Kenya, and Mozambique – Use of breast milk for poisons in the eye.*

In Zimbabwe, Kenya and Mozambican communities, breast milk of breast feeding mothers has always been used to clean away poisons in the eyes especially when the poisons are from particular trees such as mukondekonde (euphorbia). When the poison enters the eye, a breast feeding mother is asked to spread her breast milk right in the eye of the victim. In no time, the eye will be cleared of the poison.

Lesson learnt: This shows that some traditional methods of treating eye problems are equally or even more effective than the Western biased eye treatments. Besides, they are more cost effective as compared to most of the Western biased medicines. (**Source:** *Personal communication. Also see Mwadime 1999 for the same use of breast milk in Kenya*).

Case Thirty-three

Application: *Zimbabwe and western Mozambique – Use of animal (such as chameleon) movements to predict future events when travelling.*

In Zimbabwe and Western parts of Mozambique movements of particular animals are used to predict future events especially by travellers. If a chameleon, for example, passes by a traveller this is interpreted as bad omen. This is interpreted otherwise when a traveller passes by before the chameleon crosses his/her path. Movements of other animals such as mongoose (*hovo/chikovo* in Shona) also carry similar interpretations. When a *hovo*, for instance, crosses over one's path only once this is interpreted as a good omen. It is bad omen if the *hovo* crosses one's path twice. So are the monkey and the baboon. When one of these crosses your path once it is interpreted as good omen, but when it crosses twice it is interpreted as bad omen. Such ways of knowing or warning signals of what may happen in the imminent future are normally used by the people in Mozambique and Zimbabwe to determine any preventive measure, prepare for mitigation and decide on the course of action by travellers. Travellers, for instance, may help avoiding accidents if the movements of such animals as those mentioned above are carefully observed.

Lesson learnt: This shows that there are many ways of knowing. Indigenous knowledge of movements of certain animals can, for example, be used to predict the future. Such ways of knowing or warning signals of what may happen in the imminent future are used to determine any preventive measures, prepare for mitigation and decide on the course of action of the travellers in terms of planning and preparing for situations ahead of them. Besides, they are more cost effective than Western scientific ways of knowing. (*Source: Personal communication*).

Lessons and concluding remarks

The cases cited above are a clear testimony that if IKs are taken seriously in issues of community development, they can go a long way in promoting sustainable development. As argued by Veitayaki (2002: 401), "traditional knowledge illustrate(s) how the traditional people learned to cope and survive within their environment". From these case studies and picking it from Veitayaki, I argue that communities are banks of knowledge: yet unlike commercial banks which invest in money, communities invest in knowledge for self-sustenance and community development.

Also, given that "many IK systems (*especially from the African continent*) are currently at risk of extinction because of the rapid natural environments and economic, political, and cultural changes on a global scale" (World Bank 1998: 7, emphasis original), there is no doubt that globalisation as understood from a Western perspective (or to mean anything from the West) is threatening the continued existence of IKs in Africa. Elsewhere (Mawere 2012), I raised the issue of the negative impacts of the so-called globalisation to African

IKSs, in particular children's traditional games that are fast disappearing from their societies of origin due to the disastrous impacts of globalisation. This is not to say that globalisation per se or as an all-encompassing process is negative: globalisation becomes negative as soon as cultures and values of other people (especially Westerners) are imposed on others (especially Africans) such that the latter are forced to abandon their own. I emphasise once again in this book that IK can vanish from the scene if a negative attitude by advocators of a narrow view of globalisation – globalisation that looks down upon other cultures and values – continues as was in Africa since the advent of colonialism. There is, therefore, need for a change of attitude by the Western scholars and all those who advocate for globalisation to ensure that all cultures are equally considered and without discrimination or favour for foreign technologies and development concepts when it comes to knowledge and development studies across Africa and also other parts of the world.

Chapter 4

Technological Knowledge as a Component of Indigenous Knowledge Systems: The Resilience of African Science

As described by National Research Foundation (NRF) (2000) of South Africa, indigenous knowledge systems (IKSs) (or what I call African indigenous sciences) are a complex set of knowledge and technologies existing and developed around specific conditions of populations and communities indigenous to a particular geographical area. Mondal (2009) made more or less the same characterisation when he maintains that indigenous knowledge system (IKS) could be divided into various domains like agriculture, animal husbandry (including poultry and fishery), handicrafts, tools and techniques (technology), nutrition, health care practices and bio-medicines, psycho-social care, natural and biological resource, management of environmental and bio-diversity resources, disaster mitigation, human resource management, saving and lending, poverty alleviation and community development as well as education and communication; each of these domains is provided with own respective area and manifestation. Similarly, Das Gupta (2011: 62) explains that indigenous knowledge system is a multidisciplinary subject as it consists of the following dimensions: physical sciences and related technologies, social sciences and humanities. All these descriptions or characterisations suffice to argue that technological knowledge is part and parcel of indigenous knowledge systems which are in turn embedded in culture. In this chapter, I focus more on indigenous technologies that are

81

embedded in the indigenous knowledge systems in different societies across the continent of Africa, how these technologies have evolved over time, and how they can promote sustainable development in Africa and even beyond.

Understanding Technology

The concept of technology like many other concepts that are philosophical in nature has never been easy to pin down such that scholars do not universally agree on the meaning of the referred concept. For this reason, some scholars like Bijker, Hughes and Pinch (1987) have suggested that it is pointless for scholars to labour on working out precise definitions of technology as a precise definition of the referred is bound to fail given that technology has no single universally agreed upon meaning. Almost a decade later, scholars such as Fellows (1995: 1) echoed similar sentiment as demonstrated in the introduction to his edited book of essays on philosophy of technology where he notes that "the contributors to this volume do not concern themselves with the essentialist exercise of defining technology; they more or less take it for granted that the reader is familiar with a variety of technologies, such as Information Technology and proceed from there". In the recent years, other scholars like Lawson (2008) have warned that attempts to provide definition(s) of technology are generally accepted as either futile or perilous. This shows that there are serious controversies surrounding the concept of technology as a concept and technology studies as a discipline, yet in social science texts just like in education/curriculum policy documents, it is fundamentally important that definitions are given so as to be able to draw lines around the issue under discussion. It is in view of this realisation that attempts to provide definitions for the concept of technology have persevered and continue a necessity though come from different angles and disciplines.

In theorising the issue of technology, Michael Foucault (1988), suggested that technology be categorised into four broad areas namely technologies of the self, that is, the study of the ethics of the individual; technologies of sign systems, that is, those that permit human beings to use symbols, signs or meanings; technologies of power, that is, those that determine individual behaviour; and technologies of production that allow human beings to produce, transform or manipulate things. According to Foucault, these four types of technologies always function together but they are not reducible to one another as each type is associated with a certain domination (see also Burkitt 2002). Burkitt (2002: 224), in line with Foucault wrote in his paper titled: *Technologies of the self: Habitus and capacities,* the following about technology:

Technology is a form of practical action accompanied by practical reason, which aims to instil in the body certain habitual actions—either moral virtues (that is, right ways of acting in a situation) or technical skills—and, later, to give people the reflexive powers to reason about their virtues or skills, providing them with the capacity to refine, modify or change them. In other words, technology is a means through which humans produce not only products and works, but also themselves as human selves in both their reflexive and non-reflexive aspects. It is through various technologies that humans develop the habits, capacities, skills, identity, and knowledge that mark them out as individual members of a social and cultural group.

I argue in this book that while Burkitt's definition of technology focuses much on the self (technology of the self), the understanding of technology in community development and curriculum policy documents focus more on the practical nature of technology as well as the relationship between technology and humans. In this relationship, technology is conceived as a means to satisfy the needs and wants of human beings and the society concerned. Considering this view, the Standards for Technological Literacy (International Technology Education Association (2002: 2)), defines technology in the practical sense of the word as:

> *How people modify the natural world to suit their own purposes. From the Greek word techné, meaning art or artifice or craft, technology literally means the act of making or crafting, but more generally it refers to the diverse collection of processes and knowledge that people use to extend human abilities and to satisfy human needs and wants.*

Similarly, from the International Technology Education Association's conception of technology, the South African Department of Education (2002: 4, emphasis original) develops its definition of technology as:

> *The use of knowledge, skills, and resources to meet people's needs and wants by developing practical solutions to problems, taking social and environmental factors into consideration* during the use of the knowledge, skills, and resources in solving the problems in question.

While the South African Department of Education's definition of technology is somehow similar to the

International Technology Education Association's definition, differences still exist. The major difference between the two is that the latter emphasises much on the social and environmental factors rather than the practical skills per se. Yet the key tenets in these two definitions remain their emphasis on humans' relationship with technology, the influence or impact of culture on creativity, social environment as well as indigenous knowledge on development and use of the technologies. These key tenets also echo with the Greek etymology of the concept of technology, that is, *'techné'* which was used to refer to the arts, crafts or skill (know-how). As such, though the concept of technology has become dynamic and difficult to pin down, it was this sense in which 'technology' refers to a body of knowledge about the useful arts that prevailed from Renaissance times well into the industrial era (Misa 2003) and even today.

Yet understood from a practical sense as this, technology remains a terrain normally conflated with and sometimes confused with science; hence the need to distinguish the two. Science and technology are closely related but do not mean one and the same thing: their relationship is complex. As Adams (1991) and Vandeleur (2010: 14) pointed out, "when the two [science and technology] first became related, science followed technology: for example, thermodynamics followed the invention of the steam engine. However, more recently, scientific discoveries have been the basis for technological developments, such as lasers, and nuclear fission and fusion". This entails that the idea that science leads to technology and not vice-versa is a relatively recent one, and the two are different. Neither is technology a subset of science but an autonomous and distinctive field from science (Gardner

1994; Compton & France 2007). In distinguishing science from technology, Compton (2004) suggested three key characteristics namely: their purpose, their ontological stance and their epistemology. Compton further argues that the role of scientists is to quiz or interrogate the concrete/'real things' of the natural world in order to explain and make a human-mediated representation or claim about them. In this whole process of the scientific inquiry, new knowledge and consensus [as truth] about that knowledge is created through empirical verification, validation and logical reasoning. Unlike science, technological knowledge has the process of function as its reference point such that it is validated on the basis of its success in dealing with given tasks or problems. Feenberg (2006) also views science and in particular philosophy of science as a field dealing mainly with method [scientific] and how [explanatory] truth is established, whereas technology and in particular philosophy of technology deals with utility [usefulness] and control of tasks or problems: technology intervenes in the world to produce something different (totally or partially) from that which already exists. This shows that even though science and technology are distinguishable, they are closely related to each other as both use the same rationality and philosophical foundation, that of empirical verification/observation and causality. Besides, they complement each other given that scientific knowledge and methodologies, for example, are a major source of input into technological development and results. This means that science in a way has key tools for determining the success of technological interventions. Similarly, technological practices, knowledge and outcomes, on the other hand, provide mechanisms for science to gain a better view of its defined world (Compton 2004); hence the complimentary relationship between science and technology.

The integration of indigenous technology in development projects and education curricula in Africa

Julius Nyerere's sentiments on Western education in Africa are critical to use as the opening words for this section. Following his experiences as a critical thinker, educator, pan-Africanist, and African political analyst and leader, Nyerere (1968: 278) had this to say:

> *At present our pupils learn to despise even their own parents because they are old-fashioned and ignorant; there is nothing in our existing educational system which suggests to the pupil that he [she] can learn important things about farming from his [her] elders. The result is that he [she] absorbs beliefs about witchcraft before he [she] goes to school, but does not learn the properties of local grasses; he [she] absorbs the taboos from his family but does not learn the methods of making nutritious traditional foods. And from school he [she] acquires knowledge unrelated to agricultural life. He [she] gets the worst of both systems!*

In the passage above, Nyerere talks about the central dilemmas that the African child, since the advent of missionaries and colonialism in Africa, faces both at home and in the Western based education system he [she] receives at school. He laments that socialisation both at home and school is fast changing unfortunately for the worse in African terms as the African *indigenous literacy* skills are being shunned away due to the influence of Westernisation. I should add that in these Western-based education systems, speaking fluently in a foreign language (English), for instance, is normally mistaken for intelligence. It is in light of such realisations that I argue in view of indigenous technologies that due to the lasting impact of colonialism as well as the tide of globalisation that have swept across the African continent over the years, many indigenous technologies just like indigenous knowledge where these are constituents, are at a great risk of becoming extinct. Globalisation or rather the intrusion of Western values, development concepts and technologies in Africa are normally blamed for the fast changing economic, political, cultural, and environmental changes on the continent and even at a global scale. Such intrusions are resulting in the daunting of practices indigenous to many societies across Africa and even beyond (for example in the middle east) as the practices are overwhelmed or become inappropriate for new challenges at hand. What remains worrying, however, is that these values, concepts, skills, and technologies that are imposed on Africa in the name of globalisation, in most cases promise short-term benefits and solutions to the problems at hand as they are never capable of containing the problems for a long time: in many instances, the values are criticised for extending or creating even more problems than they intended to solve. In fact, the values, skills and technologies imposed on Africa are blamed by some analysts for planting the seed of poverty in Africa. Steve Biko (1978) makes the same point when he argues in the context of South Africa and African continent in general that poverty and destitution are not endemic to Africa, but a product of colonialism. Biko (1978: 43), thus, maintains that "poverty was a foreign concept" in pre-colonial Africa. I second Biko's argument considering the set-up and philosophy of life by the indigenous Africans during pre-colonial era. Through ubuntu, Africans emphasised the need and importance of living and working together as well as embracing the values of unity, harmony and peace with each other and the environment. People worked together in *jakwara/nhimbe* (that is, beer work parties as in the case of indigenous Africans in west-central Mozambique and in many parts of Zimbabwe), assisted passers-by and strangers (or those in need) with food, and helped the physically challenged to cultivate their fields. Such gestures ensured that no one would suffer from hunger, worse still considered as poor: communalism, thus, prevailed. This gives credit to the indigenous technologies and indigenous knowledge systems in general as these are normally resilient and of immediate practical value especially to those communities that have developed them and make a living through or out of them.

Given that there are many cultures in Africa, it is beyond dispute that Africa is endowed with indigenous materials and technologies that if harnessed could relieve the continent of its environmental, political and socio-economic related problems and advance communities' development. The harnessing of such technologies would relieve Africa from the burden of relying too much on Western modes of production that require 'modern' materials, tools and equipment that in most cases are too expensive or rather difficult to acquire. It is in light of this observation that I argue and call for the inclusion of indigenous technologies and culture in the education curricula and development projects across Africa as a hallmark for sustainable development on the continent. As Odora Hospers (2002) noted, such a call as this comes at a time when questions are being asked on the formation of knowledge production, the gap between formal institutions and society, and the vacuum in theorisation of poverty and other development related issues. De Walt (1994: 123, emphasis original), concurs when he offers "arguments for greater attention of IKS as based on the need to:

♦Create more appropriate and environmentally friendly technologies;

♦Empower people to have greater *freedom to* control their own destinies;

♦Create technologies that would have more just socio-economic, *environmental and political* implications."

I should be quick, however, to underline that my call for harnessing indigenous technologies should not be mistaken to mean doing away with all Western-based/related technologies. In fact, in my call for the serious consideration of indigenous technologies, I argue with De Beer and Whitlock (2009) that given the colonial history of the continent and now the so-called globalisation, Africa cannot avoid becoming part of what the West has achieved in the world (mainly through domination and subjugation of other cultures), but she [Africa] *shouldn't* forget that she, too, has something to offer from her own cultures and indigenous knowledge systems. Keeping on depending on or letting the West and America imposing their technologies on Africa would be disastrous for the development and socio-economic freedom of the continent. No wonder, as soon as many African countries are economically sanctioned or have economic sanctions imposed on them by the West and America, they fall on their knees: this is largely because of the continued partial to total dependence of Africa on the West and America on almost all modes of production and socio-economic survival. I content, therefore, that Africa should move swiftly from the colonial myths that she [Africa] was a *tabula rasa* before the colonial era and Western cultural systems of knowledge and production were regarded as the sole means to be used in determining the value of Africa's ideas, beliefs and general way of life (see also Ntuli 1999). I stress that Africa had its own knowledge forms/science, modes of production, ideas/philosophies of life, technological and scientific constructs that should be salvaged, developed and carried over into the future for purposes of real socio-economic and political freedom. This is beyond doubt as many scholars, through research and theorisation, have alluded to the same notion. As the archaeologists, Huffman (1971) and Garlake (1982a), for example pointed out, there is ample evidence that iron smelting was taking place on the African continent and especially in what is present day Zimbabwe, as early as between AD 200-600, long before the British and other Europeans harboured on the African shores. But as Garlake (1982b: 4) rightfully noted, the White colonial regime "was determined to denigrate and diminish traditional culture. It [White colonial regime] recognised that Great Zimbabwe was a powerful symbol for a rising nationalist movement....and complex economy based on the efficient management of local resources" as well as mining and trading. Even renowned European scholars like Randles (1979) have clearly acknowledged that at the height of the Portuguese interaction with the Shona people on the Zimbabwean Plateau, the Shona were already technologically well advanced and become specialists in metallurgy that some of the produce of their labour was bought by the Portuguese for re-exportation to Genoa in India to make guns, among other things. The enormous and numerous stone structures of the Great

Zimbabwe type (in Zimbabwe), the gorgeous architectural Great Pyramids of Egypt, and the great art works of the so-called Khoisan of Botswana are other excellent examples that exemplify the wisdom, scientific and technological advancement that Africa had already made well before the advent of colonialism on the continent. Such knowledge was not only unique to Zimbabwe, Egypt, and Botswana, but pervasive across the continent as there is ample evidence that the ancient African kingdoms, far and near, related with each other in many different ways. This is confirmed by Herbert Wendt (1970), Randles (1979), Garlake (1982a), and Bhebe (2000), among other scholars. Herbert Wendt cited in Jackson (1970), for example, notes that: "The dynasty of the 'Rulers of the Mines' was a Negro one. Its culture, customs, civilisation, clearly resembles those of Egypt. Marriage between royal brothers and sisters, the princesses' complete freedom in love, the sacrifices of first fruits – these are the only a few parallels between Egypt and the Shona kingdom. The connections between the Nile and Zambezi are so striking, between the land of Punt and the mining of the later Zimbabwe, are so numerous that it is difficult to discount the Egyptian contacts with southern Africa". Other structures that pre-colonial Africa takes pride in are Mapungubwe in South Africa and Manekweni in Mozambique (Garlake 1992). It should, therefore, be underscored that the rich African indigenous knowledge and technologies, resilient as they are, still exist in many parts of the continent and should be tapped and integrated into the mainstream development projects and education curricula across countries for the good of the people of Africa and beyond. Yet barriers remain on the way for the smooth integration of indigenous technologies in development projects and education curricula in Africa due to the continued influence of the Euro-American values in the name of globalisation.

Some barriers to integrating indigenous technologies in development projects and education curricula in Africa

Considering the potential contribution of indigenous technology to community development and poverty alleviation, the integration of indigenous knowledge, and in particular indigenous technology in education curricula and for development interventions in Africa is fundamentally important. Yet, there are barriers for use of indigenous technology to development interventions in general and in education curricula in particular in many education systems across Africa. Exploring and understanding these barriers is necessary in order to determine how they can possibly be overcome for purposes of sustainable development and socio-economic and political freedom in Africa. Some of the barriers to the use and integration of indigenous technologies in development interventions and education curricula in many African countries include the following:

♦ *Dominance of Western technology*
Western technologies throughout the world have been awarded higher status than technologies from many other parts of the world (commonly known as indigenous epistemologies) such as Africa. This has been mainly due to the long lasting impacts of Western colonialism and racial slavery in many parts of the world, especially in Africa. Recently, the dominance of Western technology on Africa has been exacerbated by globalisation that has eroded African cultural values including indigenous technologies. Writing

about the impact of globalisation on Africa, Maweu (2011: 36, emphasis original) argues that:

> *The advent of globalisation in Africa, with its emphasis on modern science and technology, has led to this form of knowledge being either subsumed in the western concept of 'knowledge for sustainable development', or ignored altogether. The irony is that most of the developments in science and technology, which are at the core of globalisation and "civilisation", have their roots in indigenous knowledge* given that all knowledge forms are basically grounded in locally-generated ethnoknowledge.

Such a realisation in the last couple of decades, that most technological advancements have their roots in indigenous knowledge, has resulted in the need by many development agencies to seriously consider the status and contribution of indigenous technologies to development. In fact, the need to reconsider the contribution of indigenous knowledges and technologies has been manifested at global level through development organisations such as the World Bank, among others. Nevertheless, the problem remains that seldom in the history of development agencies and education curricula in Africa has laws been amended so quickly to ensure smooth rapid integration of indigenous technologies in development interventions and education curricula. As such, there are always challenges in integrating indigenous technologies in development agents and education curricula. This is the point that Taylor and de Loë (2012) alluded to when they observed that policy makers, practitioners, scientists and other stakeholders all have epistemological challenges related to integrating local knowledge into adaptation projects. This has been chiefly a result of the widespread belief, since colonialism in Africa, that scientific technology is superior to indigenous technology: indigenous technologies just like indigenous knowledge systems themselves have been despised and their potentials undermined. Blaikie, Brown, Stocking, Tang, Dixon, and Sillitoe (1997) hammer the same point when they argue that the main challenge in integrating indigenous technologies in the mainstream development interventions is that development professionals are not pragmatic in outlook and exercise power to defend their superiority through specialisation, rejection of alternative knowledge, and assimilation in the name of professional excellence. This is possibly because indigenous technologies are in a way seen as potential threats to current dominant technologies used in development regimes. Such an observation as this cannot be easily denied given the Western tendencies since colonialism, tendencies to denigrate and despise African ways of knowing, technologies and medicines. In colonial Zimbabwe, for example, it is well documented that for missionaries and colonial government to outcompete traditional healers, they labelled traditional medicines as dirty, superstitious and classified them under witchcraft (see also Chavunduka 1980).

♦ *Inaccessibility to indigenous technologies*

The other barrier to the integration of indigenous technologies into the mainstream education curricula and development agencies in Africa is the limited accessibility by development and education professionals to some of the technologies. More often than not, indigenous technologies are inaccessible due to difficulty in comprehension, documentation, validation, integration, transmission, and application by education technocrats and development experts. The aforementioned factors even aggravate when a particular thread of indigenous technologies is held by dominant group of a given community who may be unwilling to share it for common good and like to hold it privately. Sometimes, the inaccessibility of indigenous technologies result from issues related to property rights which in many cases are unclear when it comes to indigenous technologies or indigenous knowledge systems in general.

♦Limited time and information by researchers

Indigenous technologies belong to particular communities. This means that in order to tap and integrate these technologies into the mainstream education curriculum or development projects, there is need for a 'sustainable' dialogue, understanding and negotiations between 'experts' and all stakeholders involved. Successful dialogue and negotiation in such deals would certainly require adequate information about each other – between experts and the owners of the indigenous technologies – as well as the establishment of faith and trust between the referred. Thus as Blaikie, Brown, Stocking, Tang, Dixon, and Sillitoe (1997) suggested, successful dialogue and negotiation in such deals require longer period [of experts] in the field with expensive transaction costs than development agencies and education professionals want to spend: in most cases, there is therefore information and time deficit. To break through this problem, I therefore argue that development experts and education technocrats alike should fully commit themselves and engage in a sustainable dialogue with the traditional owners and users of indigenous technologies in order to tap and integrate them (into curricular and education development projects) for the common good.

♦Implementation Planning Flaws

In many development projects and education curricula in Africa, the formulation of plans for implementation are often top-down and rarely draw on local/indigenous technologies or indigenous knowledge systems in general at planning phase. A good rapport and course of action are not built into the development and curricula at the design stage. This is planning flaw. As noted by scholars such as Parlee (2012) and Nakashima, Galloway-McLean, Thulstrup, Ramos-Castillo, and Rubis (2012), planning flaw is often the result of other barriers that range from financial, technical and capacity issues associated with the documentation of appropriate traditional knowledge and participation of communities, to more deeply rooted problems of social relations, trust, and power. All these factors, thus, are barriers to the integration of indigenous technologies into the mainstream development projects and education curricula in many African societies, and they need to be carefully addressed to ensure sustainable development.

Chapter 5

Leveraging Sustainable Development in the Twenty-First Century Africa: A Critical Dialogue

In chapter three of this book, I captured and elaborated on a considerable amount of indigenous knowledges (IKs) around the African continent. This was in a way to demonstrate the indispensability, applicability and transferability of IKs within and across societies. Yet even with all these demonstrations, the problem of how and whether IKs as well as indigenous technologies (ITs) embedded within indigenous knowledge systems (IKSs) could really be integrated for community development as independent alternative forms of knowledge or even a compliment of Western science in this age of the so-called globalisation remains topical. This question is topical in the twenty-first century given the sad history of IKSs, particularly in Africa since the dawn of colonialism. It is also topical considering the continued persistence of many problems that Western scientific knowledge (SK) alone has failed to tackle and provide solution to since it [SK] started its hegemonic monopoly as the only true knowledge the world over. In the next section, I discuss the divide between SK and IK that was created by the Western 'modernists', and how we can go beyond the divide in our attempt to foster sustainable development and socio-economic and political freedom in the twenty-first century Africa.

Rethinking the epistemological divide between [Western] Scientific Knowledge (SK) and indigenous knowledge (IK)

Since colonialism, Africa has been described as a dark continent with the African people's culture, norms and values, and indigenous knowledge labelled as savagery, superstitious, barbaric, and relegated to oblivion as irrational and unscientific. It is in view of these misrepresentations of Africa and the African people mostly by missionaries and Eurocentric scholars that Europe saw herself as a redeemer who on God's behalf had the obligation to come and deliver Africa from this one whole night of savagery, superstition, and barbarism (see also Achebe 1958). As Kunnie (2005) puts it, European colonisation was viewed [by the colonialists] as a way of "civilising uncivilised savage Africans" in line with the "white man's burden" of European enlightenment of redeeming the globe from barbaric self-destruction. This looking down upon Africa led the missionaries and Western colonialists to label the African people as the 'other' distinct from themselves [Europeans] in all respects. As such, the African indigenous knowledges which the African people believed to be embedded in their culture and acted as the source of their [Africans] ambitions and creativity as well as development were considered superstitious, despised and relegated as unscientific in the Western modernist sense of the word science. To make sure that any form of knowledge associated with the African people, practices and values was distinguished from the Western people's form(s) of knowledge, the European bulwark of colonialism set binaries between the knowledge forms by the Africans and those by the Westerners. The words 'indigenous knowledge' and 'science,' thus, were coined to distinguish the two. The former was used derogatorily to refer to any form of knowledge, practices and beliefs held by the African people. The practicability and value of those knowledge forms, practices and beliefs to those who owned and used them was never considered. On the other hand, the word 'science' was used to designate any form of knowledge associated with the Westerners and the global/universal. The Europeans, thus, appropriated science and claimed it unjustifiably as the unique baby of their own making. This does not mean to say that the Europeans didn't know that Africans had their own science. Europeans only wanted to monopolise science and knowledge in general as well as to justify their claim that Africa has no history worse still science. No wonder why those scholars who argue from a Eurocentric perspective consider the word 'indigenous knowledge' derogatory even when used by the Africans and from the African people's perspective. I will not pursue this discussion here as I have pursued it elsewhere except to say that I consider the word African 'indigenous knowledge' appropriate as long as it is used from the perspective of the African people and not from the perspective of the [former] colonialists and Eurocentric scholars. Also, I remain convinced that IK just like Western SK should be viewed as a global or universal heritage and resource as it can also be globally appreciated (Vilakazi 1999), and could be used to benefit people of other communities anywhere in the world (where applicable). Yet, while this was important to point out, this chapter is committed to rethink the binaries between indigenous knowledge and science – binaries that were set by Western modernists to distinguish their knowledge (which they perceived as superior) from that of the rest (which they believed to be inferior). Let us, therefore, try to find out how the binaries (of indigenous knowledge and Western science) have been conceptualised by some scholars over the years. I should not promise that I will look at what all scholars who have grappled with the question of IK – science dichotomy say, but will just focus on a handful of these scholars in an effort to generate discussion, and to provide insights into how the binary between science and indigenous knowledge could be rethought and the 'gap' bridged. In order to do this, I choose to focus on the science – IK debate that has and continues to take place in the circles of anthropology of knowledge and environmental anthropology.

Over the years, the discourse on the epistemological divide between science and other knowledge forms, particularly the so-called 'indigenous knowledge' (IK) has become highly momentous and has sustained controversies of epic proportions in anthropology of knowledge and conservation sciences/environmental anthropology. Given the nebulous nature of IK coupled with the different interpretations evoked by the deployment of the concept across different cultures and disciplines, a robust comprehension of the concept in terms of how it relates to other forms of knowledge such as Western scientific knowledge generally referred to in this book as science, calls into question its practical manifestations and application in particular situated contexts such as those of anthropology of knowledge and environmental anthropology. I should point out that more often than not, in these contexts, positivists and Eurocentric modern scientists tend not only to draw a solid line between science and IK, but also favour science and undermine the possible contribution of IK. They seem not to understand that indigenous knowledge is embedded in the respective cultural environments and histories of all people across the world, Europeans included. In fact there is no way we can deny the fact that people are historically and culturally bound and thus have a peculiar knowledge system, which enables them not only to survive, but also to become a civilised community (Vilakazi 1999; Ntuli 1999). This is the point that positivists and modern Eurocentric scientists seem to have missed and indeed continue to miss; hence they embrace what they call 'science' and distance themselves from what they call 'indigenous knowledge'. Yet in the recent years, the failure by science to solve most of the problems facing humanity such as environmental problems has provoked critical researchers to rethink the modernist indigenous knowledge – science dualism. The rethinking has been and is being done, but with little progress due to complexities surrounding the dualism. The complexity of establishing a concrete solution to the dualism or 'divide' between science and indigenous knowledge is summed up in Green's (unpublished manuscript: 1) assertion that "although Euro – American philosophy cannot possibly be considered the sum of human intellectual heritage, the contrary remains the dominant assertion in most university – based scholarship….and several paradoxes trouble many of the vital ideas/claims made in the name of indigenous knowledge systems". The complexity thus persists even to date.

On one hand, some scholars argue for the dominance of science over other knowledge heritages such as indigenous knowledge (IK). Kai Horsthemke (2008, 2010), for example, argues for the valorisation and dominance of science in so far as for him science is universal and other knowledge forms are not: for him, it is only to modern science that we must turn in our efforts to address the most pressing issues of our time such as HIV/Aids, environmental degradation and global warming. In one of his pieces, Horsthemke (2008: 129) argues that "indigenous knowledge involves at best an incomplete, partial or, at worst, a questionable understanding or conception of knowledge; and, that as a tool in anti-discrimination and anti-repression discourse, 'indigenous knowledge' is largely inappropriate". As one scholar arguing for a universalist position on knowledge issues, Horsthemke is of the view that there is no valid reason why we should argue for commensurability of diverse epistemologies. This is because "when one account is true and another false, or one is adequately justified and another only insufficiently so, it is fairly clear which one ought to be favoured, on epistemological grounds" (Horsthemke 2010: 4). As such, Horsthemke advances [strict] realism given that for him, "the only coherent and consistent position is a realist view of the pertinent issues and ideas; *Western* science is a privileged way of seeing the world" (ibid: 1, emphasis original). His argument is criticised by Green (2008, 2009). Though agreeing with Horsthemke to some extent, for example, that defining what is 'indigenous' about IK is somehow complex as indigenous people are always in contact with others, Green is against both Horsthemke's realism – the belief that "there is a reality that is not dependent on thought or language, a world that exists independently of me, the researcher, the subject of inquiry" [see Pring 2004] – and relativism. Relativism is the belief that ways of knowing the world depend on where we come from i.e. our cultural contexts. Instead of following Horsthemke's universalist position, Green proposes to proffer a different answer to the question by arguing that diverse epistemologies ought to be evaluated not on the basis of strict realism, but on their ability to advance understanding. In her words, "positions within the sciences about epistemology are heavily contested and the production of an absolute, universal truth is rejected" (Green 2009: 42). At least in this respect, Green's approach (unlike Horsthemke's) has the merit that "it allows all 'workable' beliefs [*like most indigenous knowledges*] as well as those that pass the Western epistemic test [like scientific knowledge which according to Elgin (2004) is not 'true' in the strict sense of the term] to be considered as valid" (Green 2008:154, emphasis original). Put differently, where knowledge diversity is recognised no knowledge form is marginalised simply because it fails to pass the epistemic test – the fulfilments of objective/Western scientific knowledge. Instead, all people/cultures have the opportunity to use their day-to-day experiences and practices in the production of knowledge and advancement of understanding. All this is enough to say that Horsthemke's anthropology of knowledge fails to move beyond the IK – Science divide. Horsthemke's argument also falls short in that it fails to take into cognisance the fact that "the field of epistemology is not limited to universalism and relativism as neither these theories are satisfactory foundations for knowledge" (see Green 2008: 147).

More so, Horsthemke's realism amounts to the poor habits of "Othering" and "Saming" both of which "are poor substitutes for understanding and explaining" (Green, unpublished manuscript: 5) human societies/cultures. "Othering" is the practice of comparing oneself to the other(s) while at the same time distancing from the later – the other (Lacan 1964). In Othering, the one who is making the comparison puts himself/herself in a superior position (or a high moral ground) than the other such that distance between the two is always maintained. This is opposed to "Saming" which is the practice of comparing oneself to the other (s) with the intention to disempower, dominate and influence him/her to be "just like me" (Green, Unpublished manuscript :5) or else suffer isolation or remain marginalised and disadvantaged. Both Othering and Saming are negative given that they have the undesirable consequence of cultivating "hierarchical or stereotypical thinking" (ibid) and consequently amounts to a narrow way of understanding and interpreting societal/cultural realities.

On the other hand, scholars like Thokozani Xaba argue for the opposite – dominance of indigenous knowledge over Western science. Xaba (2008) grappling with the question on the anthropology of knowledge, particularly within the context of South African debate on traditional medicines and the sciences, challenges the monopoly of science as the predominant way of accessing, communicating and transmitting knowledge. He argues for "cognitive justice" as the only way to redress the marginalisation of other knowledge heritages brought about by the twin projects of colonialism and Western modernity (see also Green 2009). Cognitive justice is a critique of the dominant paradigm of Western modern science which aims at promoting the full recognition of alternative forms of knowledge by facilitating and enabling a democratic and sustainable dialogue between science and other forms of knowledge (Boaventura de Sousa 2007; Visvanathan 2009). For Xaba, redressing this problem (of Science's relationship with other knowledge forms) is critical because "it corrects the misconception that development still largely refers to the westernisation of the world thereby making the rest of the world conform to the economic, socio-cultural, and political norms that have developed in the 'West'" (Xaba 2008: 319, emphasis original).

Yet, while Xaba rightly argues for 'cognitive justice' through compare and contrast of scientific and indigenous medicines, he goes on to criticise all "epistemological foundations of the worldview that is considered scientific" (Xaba 2008: 318) in the Western sense in favour of the indigenously defined epistemologies. This makes his conception of cognitive justice the direct opposite of that discussed above in view of Horsthemke, therefore radical and unconvincing. Xaba's anthropology of knowledge (like that of Horsthemke discussed before) is in sharp contrast with 'symmetrical anthropology' – an anthropology interested equally in the remote and traditional as much as the centre and the so-called modern (see Latour 1993, 2007). Thus, though he begins his piece in a noble manner that seems embracing knowledge democratisation and pluralism, Xaba's denunciation of science as helpless in dealing with South Africa's current HIV/Aids crisis is fundamentally mistaken. His [Xaba] uncritical denialist position is in agreement with the position which the former South African President, Thabo Mbeki, held when between 2000 and 2005 he failed to roll out HIV/Aids drugs to HIV patients resulting in 330,000 unnecessary deaths and the infection of 3,500 infants with HIV (Nattrass 2009). In view of this observation, it is my contention that by failing to account for the emergence of knowledge pluralism, Xaba ended up reinforcing dichotomies he set out to destabilise and dismantle – that is, the dominance of one form of knowledge, 'Othering' and 'Saming'. In fact since attempts to deal with HIV/Aids have been unsuccessful because of (among other reasons) science's failure to pay attention to other knowledge forms, a sensible move would be to embrace other knowledge heritages in dealing with our current pressing health as well as such other problems.

In view of the possible criticisms that could be levelled against the two warring positions explicated above, more other scholars like James Fairhead and Melissa Leach (1995) have argued in a somewhat different direction from that of Horsthemke and Xaba. Arguing for "a democratic and sustainable dialogue" (Boaventura 2007) between science and other forms of knowledge or a somewhat "reflective equilibrium" (to use Catherine Elgin's (2004) phrase) – an approach that moves beyond the IK-Science divide, Fairhead and Leach question the dominance of science and perceptions about its opaqueness to the public which have "led to a focus on 'back-end' consequences such as risk, in effect protecting the broader trajectory of scientific and technological development from accountability" (Davies et al 2009: 340). For them, this raises critical questions about whether different forms of knowledge cannot be developed (in universities and beyond) outside the terms and parameters defined by science. What is lost in the process of moving from conventional scientific inquiry towards the unorthodox processes of searching for other forms of knowing like examining other knowledge forms? These questions raise challenges that require new responses to the numerous problems the world is facing today. Yet, the questions cannot be adequately addressed without challenging the monopoly of science as the predominant way of accessing, communicating and transmitting knowledge. The rise in "citizen science" – participatory processes of public understanding and even the act of challenging science research is the direct consequence of public frustration with the limitations of [Western] science. To demonstrate the insufficiency of science where it is accorded the monopoly over other knowledge forms, Fairhead and Leach (1995) make reference to their ethnographic findings in West Africa around the issue of deforestation. The duo in their piece, *"False forest history…",* ethnographically examine how over the years, social science has explained the rapid and recent deforestation supposed to have occurred in Guinea, West Africa, so as to inform policy responses to it. Using two case studies namely, forest island of Kissidougou and Ziama forest reserve, Fairhead and Leach explore "the production of applied social science knowledge about people-environment relations' in Guinea which exemplify the type of social analysis often brought to bear to explain environmental degradation in Africa" (pp. 1023). For the duo, these two case studies clearly expose common assumptions [I shall elaborate in the next paragraph] on which [Western] science research on Africa tend to draw. And though these assumptions have strengths and credibility due to their systematic logic in writing and justification, "once dissected from the reality they seek to construct, they reveal how the applied social sciences can be used to lend weight to popular Western perceptions about African society and environment – a mythical reality which development interventions are acting to recreate in vain" (ibid). For this reason, Fairhead and Leach argue for the need to rethink people – environment relationships in Guinea; they call for a "diplomatic anthropology" (to use Isabelle Stengers' terminology) which puts to question both the idea of Western science and other knowledge forms as much as that of nature and culture. To justify their case – the need for critical thinking around issues of knowledge and the environment – Fairhead and Leach carry out an ethnographic research in the two areas mentioned above, Kissidougou and Ziama.

From their research, the duo observed that social scientists and policy makers or rather Eurocentric "foreign observers/scientists today tend to date [all] socio-environmental disruption [in Kissidougou and Ziama like socio-economic change, increasing mobility/migration, weakening of traditional authority, individuated farming/shifting cultivation, cultural decadence, alienation of local resource control to state structures, commercialisation of local charcoal, fuel wood and timber, and population growth] to the 'notorious' regime of Guinea's first republic (1958-84) under Sokou Toure imaging the colonial period as environmentally friendly, while nationals tend to look to the pre-colonial period to find 'good' society and environment" (pp. 1024). To further demonstrate this misconstrued conception by [foreign] observers, Fairhead and Leach cite Project Kan 11 scientists' (1992) report which states that: "At origin, the forest between Kissidougou and Kankan was.....a dense, humid, semi-deciduous forest. The trigger of degradation is...the farming system" by their shifting cultivation and fire-setting practices, preserving only the belt of forest around their villages to protect their settlements from fire and wind...and to provide seclusion for secret ritual activities" (ibid). Fairhead and Leach also cite recent research results by professional social scientists on environmental issues in Kissidougou which attributed the "the deterioration of the environment, to 'erosion and soil impoverishment, the drying up of water sources, the origin and nature of forest destruction which all result largely from 'the origin of perverse use of bush fire...and socio-economic, political, religious break-ups" (Project Kan II 1992).

Contrary to the findings of these studies, Fairhead and Leach's ethnographic study identifies with Zerouki (1993) and

110

Fofana (1993) who observed that "degradation in Guinea seems to be recent and the twin project of colonialism and 'modernity' which disrupted the once successful integration of fire control within diffuse sets of intra and inter-village social, cultural and political relationships" (Fairhead and Leach 1995: 1025). This difference between researchers on agency for environmental degradation makes the whole question of science-IK divide even more complex and difficult to unpack. For Fairhead and Leach, this complexity makes it paramount to rethink the credibility of science and to "re-examine how vegetation has actually changed in Kissidougou [using historical data sources ignored or deemed unnecessary by (some) Scientists such as aerial photographs, oral history, earlier documentary sources like explorers' reports, reviewed descriptions and maps] as a necessary first step in evaluating these social science analyses" (ibid: 1026). As Fairhead and Leach point out, historical data sources have the merit that they "cast into question the relationships between society, demography and environment" (Ibid: 1027). Also, they take into account the fact that local land use (which incorporate locally generated knowledge) can be vegetation-enriching as well as degrading (if uncontrolled). This is a balanced and bias free view.

Using these data sources in 27 of the 38 villages investigated, Fairhead and Leach produce a counter-narrative [of social scientists and policy makers'] which establishes that the forest history of Kissidougou and Ziama regions documented by social scientists and policy makers was false and ill-founded; "it is an explanation for forest loss which has not actually been taking place" (ibid). The duo established that "there has been a broadly positive relationship between the peopling of Kissidougou and Ziama and their forest

111

cover. As settlements are associated with the formation of forest islands, more villages mean more forest islands" (Ibid: 1028). For this reason, "recent approaches by state agencies [and foreign organisations], which focus on decentralising resource control by establishing village-level organisation and environmental management plans, actually risk undermining the existing flexible, diverse constellation of resource management relations"(Ibid). Fairhead and Leach thus argue for a counter-narrative with environmental policies that emphasize support to proven local practices and knowledges but without denigrating science. Their argument is in agreement with Visvanathan's (1997, 2009) "cognitive justice" with which he argues for the democratisation and diversity of knowledge for diversity's sake. Such a stance is critical as emphasis has to be placed on the need to gain the participation, acceptance and support of local populations if conservation is to be sustainable (see Fairhead and Leach 1995: 1030); otherwise "foreign and externally enforced" environmental management faces resistance. A democratic, sustainable dialogue between science and other knowledge forms thus is necessary.

Drawing on the foregoing, I argue that Fairhead and Leach's position has the merit that unlike other researchers (such as Horsthemke and Xaba discussed above) that exhaust more energies on denigrating other forms of knowledge and practices, theirs focus on locally generated environmental management practices as complimentary and alternatives to scientific environmental management practices. As Fairhead and Leach (Ibid: 1033) succinctly aver, counter-narratives such as theirs "provide different and more appropriate guidelines for policy and present socio-environmental change in a way which better fits local experience; it provides a more effective basis for a sustainable dialogue and participatory development work with local populations". As such, Fairhead and Leach's argument for the need to rethink and democratise knowledge is convincing and more appealing as it opens dialogue between Western science and other forms of knowledge (such IK) in their quest to advance understanding; it acknowledges that both locally generated knowledge forms [IKs] and scientific ones can benefit from each other in dealing with environmental as well as many other problems that haunt us today. In short, Fairhead and Leach's position is anthropologically appealing because:

i) It avoids the undesirable habits of 'Othering' and 'Saming' discussed in the preceding paragraphs and,

ii) It acknowledges that 'sustainable' production of knowledge and advancement of understanding can only be successfully achieved if particular forms of knowledge are viewed as relative and not judged by one's values or viewpoints and, if there is dialogue between different knowledge forms. To this end, I argue with Odora-Hoppers (2001:14) that when indigenous knowledge and Western scientific knowledge systems are combined and complement each other they can achieve what neither could alone. Yet barriers, as have been discussed in view of indigenous technologies, continue to derail the integration of indigenous knowledge into community development in Africa and even in development projects at global level.

Barriers to harnessing IK for development in Africa and beyond

Obsession with Western scientism

There are many barriers that impede the harnessing of IK to steer and foster development in Africa as in many other parts of the world. As can be witnessed in the discussion above, I consider the greatest obstacle to harnessing IK for development as the obsession of many scientists of the present day with Western scientism. Most of our scientists today have either been trained in the West (where they have been brainwashed) or trained in the continent but in institutions where all curricula are totally or largely Western in terms of content, methodologies and even approaches to problem solving. All what they know are therefore the Western cannons of knowledge, and still they believe Western science is superior to all other knowledge forms. This obsession has and is resulting in the continued relegation of IK to the periphery of development agendas. It is my contention, therefore, that as long as African scientists (whether natural or social scientists) continue with their obsession of Western scientism, indigenous knowledges in Africa will continue to suffer. As a matter of consequence, development on the continent will continue slowing down. There is need for African scientists to valorise their IK, improve or deploy them to solve problems where possible: what is need is indeed a change of attitude by African scientists. Once attitude towards indigenous knowledge by scientists is positive, development on the continent is likely to improve.

Lack of national institutional guidelines/policies in support of indigenous knowledge for development

In many African countries, there are no national IK institutions to protect IK and guide citizens on how these should be used. While some African countries such as South Africa, Cameroon, Nigeria, Burkina Faso, Kenya, Ghana, Zimbabwe, and Madagascar have already established IK institutions in their respective countries, majority of the countries in Africa are still far from establishing such. As observed by World Bank (1998: iii):

> *Knowledge as an instrument of development has not received the needed attention in developing countries in general and in Africa in particular. This is changing. As the awareness of the importance of knowledge in the development process grows, the next logical step would be for the country authorities to begin elaborating specific policies in support of acquiring, absorbing and communicating knowledge, with particular attention to indigenous knowledge. The partners should encourage this process through financial and technical support.*

It is my contention, therefore, that the complacency by many African countries will continue witnessing slow economic and even socio-political development on the continent.

Lack of Legal Framework

Due to lack of legal frameworks for the exploitation of IK in many African countries, many companies (transnational or national) tend to exploit IK in a way that benefit them and at the expense of the country as a whole. There is no win – win situation (between transnational companies and host countries) in the exploitation of IK in many African countries due to lack of legal frameworks that protect IKs and guide individuals or companies when exploiting IKs. Consequences for this lack of legal framework are often undesirable on the part of the host country. As noted by Tom Suchanandan, an environmental legal expert in the National Indigenous Knowledge System Office under the Department of Science and Technology:

> *The African Union did an economic study in 2005 and it revealed at that time that Africa was losing between US$5, 6 billion and US$8 billion from the theft of its biodiversity....Although it's difficult to quantify the losses, we can give indicators since 98% of patents held worldwide are held by developed countries while only 2 % are held by India and other developing countries (Sifelani Tsiko 2012: 2).*

The above makes it clear that Africa is perhaps losing even more than US$8 billion cited by Suchanandan. No African country is free from the losses. As recent as 2010, South Africa, for example, recorded two accusations of bio-piracy. Regis Mafuratidze (cited in Tsiko 2012: 2) thus reports:

> *The first 2010 South African bio-piracy case involved the illegitimate use of traditional knowledge surrounding the medicinal properties of pelargonium sidoides by Germany's Schwabe, and the second, the bio-prospecting on Honeybush and Rooibos by Swiss food giant Nestle without appropriate permits from the South African government.*

In another case on the African soils, particularly Kenya:

German pharmaceutical giant Bayer filed a patent in 1995 for the manufacture of Glucobay, a drug that treats type 11 diabetes and which was based on a bacteria strain originating from lake Ruiru in Kenya. Local communities from the Ruiru region never benefitted from the exploitation of their resources (Ibid).

Though the Convention on Biological Diversity (CBD) of 1993 and Nagoya Protocol were put in place as instruments which control the fair use and benefit of biodiversity or genetic resources, it remains clear that there is no strict system or framework to monitor bio-piracy and to regulate activities of multinationals most of which are from the North. As such, multinational companies continue to make huge profits from Africa's biological wealth but are not willing to share them with the local communities who own the biodiversity resources.

Another good example on the African soils that has sparked a lot of debate and controversy is the 1999 University of Zimbabwe vis-à-vis professor Kurt Hostettmann of Lausanne University, Switzerland case where agreement was entered in 1995 for Snake – Bean (*Mutukutu*) plant. The plant has long been used by traditional communities in Zimbabwe to treat fungal infections while the pods are used to kill snails. As reported by SEATINI (2001):

On July 27, 1999, US-patent 5'929'124 on antimicrobial diterpenes was granted to Kurt Hostettmann, professor at the University of Lausanne. The patented invention relies on traditional knowledge from Zimbabwe and on the root of the tree "Swartzia madagascariensis" that can be found throughout tropical Africa.

Two years before, in April 1997, an addendum to a material transfer and confidentiality agreement between the American pharmaceutical company Phytera and the University of Lausanne was signed, under which Phytera received an option for an exclusive worldwide license and in return agreed to pay royalties of 1.5% on the net sales of any product marketed under this license. Professor Hostettmann, on the other hand, is obliged to give 50% of any royalties received to the National Herbarium and the Botanical Garden of Zimbabwe and to the Department of Pharmacy at the University of Zimbabwe.

Hostettmann's action vis-à-vis the University of Zimbabwe was criticised by several non-governmental organisations (NGOs) including the Community Technology and Development Association (CTDA) of Zimbabwe, Zimbabwe National Traditional Healers Association (ZINATHA) and the Swiss NGO Berne Declaration on the following grounds:

i). Neither the state of Zimbabwe, nor the traditional healers affected by the bio-prospecting have been correctly informed or have given their prior informed consent for the search of genetic resources in Zimbabwe. The Convention on Biological Diversity, signed by Zimbabwe and Switzerland, states that "access to genetic resources shall be subject to prior informed consent (pic) of the contracting party providing such resources …". In Zimbabwe the mandate and the authority to allow access to genetic resources lies with the Ministry of Environment. But the Ministry never signed a contract with the University of Lausanne, nor is there any contract which shifts the mandate from the Ministry to the University of Zimbabwe, which helped the University of Lausanne to get access to the resources. The African Model legislation for the regulation of access to biological resources states that the pic of the state and the concerned local communities is needed. Part of the information requested for the pic should be the economic, social, technical, biotechnological, scientific, environmental, or any other benefits that are intended or may be likely to accrue and the proposed mechanisms and arrangements for benefit sharing.

ii). The concerned stakeholders (traditional healers, local communities, the state of Zimbabwe) were not given any of this information before the University of Lausanne gained access to genetic resources and traditional knowledge. "We have never given our consent to this deal", states Professor G. Chavunduka of the Zimbabwe National Traditional Healers Association (ZINATHA) which had submitted a number of samples of their medicines to the University of Zimbabwe for analysis. The idea was just to confirm the properties of this medicine which traditional healers in Zimbabwe have been using for time immemorial" (see also SEATINI 2001).

In short, the Zimbabwe – Switzerland case shows that there have been no mutually agreed terms for a fair and equitable benefit sharing mechanism; hence the host community (Zimbabwe) stands to lose in the whole deal. Yet cases such as the Zimbabwe – Switzerland one where the host communities are denied the right to enjoy the fruits of their own indigenous knowledge are quite numerous in developing countries and have been a problem for local communities for centuries now. As reported by Michael Blakeney (1997: 298), one of the first examples of post-colonial bio-prospecting activity is recorded from as early as the 1870's when:

Dr Bancroft, a Brisbane surgeon, used the knowledge of the Aboriginal peoples of Australia to substitute extracts from the Dubosia plant as a substitute for atropine in opthalmic cases. The plant was also found to contain hyoscine, used as a sedative, in the Second World War, a local Dubosia industry was developed, as imports of these drugs were unavailable. By the 1970's there were some 250 farmers growing Dubosia in northern New South Wales and southeast Queensland, with an export industry worth more than Aus$1 million annually. Other than in employment, the traditional users of these plants have received no tangible benefits.

All this is a clear testimony that the value of indigenous knowledge cannot be underestimated in development not only of local communities but on a global scale, yet legal framework in many countries and even at global level continue betraying and robbing local communities of their indigenous knowledges.

Lack of Basic Infrastructure in Rural Areas

In many African rural areas where indigenous knowledges are commonplace, there is lack of basic infrastructure such as road network, electricity and internet connectivity to promote the sustainable exploitation of the IKs. This makes it difficult not only to exchange indigenous knowledges between communities, but also to integrate them into the mainstream development projects. I argue, therefore, that for indigenous knowledge to be easily integrated into development projects (by external development agencies), there is need for nations to first of all develop basic infrastructure in the rural areas where most of the indigenous knowledge systems are found.

Lack of agreement between Western scientific knowledge (SK) and IK oriented professionals

In most cases the Western oriented scientists do not agree with IK oriented scientists in terms of methodologies, principles and other such modalities. For example, a common question where there is dialogue between the two is: 'To what extent do ICT professionals free from Western scientific biases towards IK and its contents and vice-versa?' The disagreement between SK biased and IK oriented professionals is mainly a result that both are fundamentalists who see no value in anything except in what they believe in. I argue, therefore, that there is need for both IK and SK fundamentalists to rethink their respective positions if there is to be a sustainable relationship between SK and IK, and also 'meaningful' development in rural communities.

Inaccessibility

In Africa, indigenous knowledge is often inaccessible to other communities or at global level due to numerous reasons including documentation, the inroads of globalisation and the exclusion of locally – based knowledge in education curricula in many schools/learning institutions across the continent. Writing about the same issue in the context of India, Prakash (2013: 31) in his report for the National Resources Management Programme in India enunciate the same reasons:

Local knowledge is often inaccessible due to difficulty in comprehension, documentation, validation, integration, transmission, and application. These factors are exacerbated locally when a particular thread of local knowledge is held by dominant group within a community who may like to hold it privately, and be

121

unwilling to share it for common good. In some cases intellectual property rights issues may also be at play.

This calls for the need for [African] countries to offer indigenous knowledge as courses in learning institutions such as colleges and universities. This would produce products or human resources with the capacity to document and evaluate indigenous knowledges in their respective communities and also explore ways of integrating them into education curricula and development projects in their communities.

Bridging the gap between different knowledges: towards sustainable dialogue between IK and SK

There is need to bridge the gap between IK and SK in order to achieve sustainable development in Africa. This will be one big step towards the dismantling and removal of the barriers surrounding the use of IK for development. There is no doubt that a sustainable dialogue between Western scientific knowledge and indigenous knowledge would accommodate worldviews and life-worlds of both SK and IK oriented individuals or groups. This knowledge interface between actors from both sides will help a great deal in promoting knowledge pluralism, enhancing the IK network capacity, and restoring the lost dignity and knowledges of the African people while at the same time accommodating those from former western imperialists. The two, SK and IK, thus, will for the first time in world history find themselves at par and forge a mutually complementing relationship that seeks to enrich each other. Such an envisioned relationship between SK and IK is possible if we are to seriously consider the observation by Flavier, De Jesus and Navarro's (1999:479, emphasis original) in their argument that indigenous knowledge is:

> *basically local knowledge that is unique to a given culture*, society or a group of people in a particular geographical location. *It is the information base for a society which facilitates communication and decision-making. As such, indigenous information systems are dynamic and continually influenced by internal creativity and experimentation, as well as by contact with external systems. Indigenous knowledge thus can easily work with other forms of knowledge* within and outside the areas they originate.

These scholars refer to indigenous knowledge as science that is user-derived, not scientifically derived in the Western sense of the word science such that its use complements and enhances the gains made by modern-day innovations and novelty. In my sense, the introduction of the concepts such as information systems and modern science as opposed to indigenous knowledge (which I consider as a science as well but not in the Western sense) seems to be pointing in the direction of regarding indigenous knowledge as made up of commodities as well as regarding indigenous knowledge systems as systems that enable the continuous integration of information and innovations whether indigenous or modern. Understood this way, then there should be no quarrel between science and indigenous knowledge: the two should be understood as compliments that both work towards problem solving and where necessary can work together to enhance each other. While the issue of problem solving seems to be obvious only in Western science where they have built laboratories for experimentation, I argue in this book that even with indigenous knowledge, experimentation is also constantly and often done in dealing with problem solving though the experiments are not explained using Western standards. This is one reason (among many others) why I consider African indigenous knowledges as African sciences. The issue of problem solving in indigenous knowledge is also underlined by Green (1996:51, emphasis original) who quoting McClure had this to say: indigenous knowledge is body of accumulated wisdom that has "evolved from years of experience, *innovative thinking,* and trial-and-error problem solving by groups of people working to meet the challenges they face in their local environments, drawing upon the resources they have at hand". I should go beyond Green, however, to argue that indigenous knowledges' function and competence is not only limited to the problem solving in environments where they (IKs) originated but can be successfully transferred and utilised in other communities, at national and global/international levels. This way, the argument by most of the Western modernist scientists that indigenous knowledge (or African science as I also call it in this book) is not a universal resource that can be equated to Western science thus doesn't hold water. In fact this kind of thinking and the continual holding on to the divisions between science and indigenous knowledge impede development in many communities, and make it extremely difficult to deal with global problems such as global warming, among others. It is my contention, therefore, that as long as we keep holding on to the Western modernist divisions between science and indigenous knowledge, and Western science remain intolerant (and even bully) to other forms of knowledge, development at community, national, continental and global levels will remain sluggish; and solving globally intriguing problems such as those to do with environment degradation, HIV/Aids, and global warming will continue a thorn in the flesh.

Chapter 6

Indigenous Knowledge, Culture and Education in Africa

In all African countries especially in south of the Sahara, pre-colonial education system was based on the culture of the society or group of people concerned: it was not education embedded in the culture of the other as is the case today in many African societies. What was most critical about this education is that it recognised the value and importance of culture especially the traditional knowledge systems that involved activities, practices, norms, and processes that were useful to the indigenous people. This being the case, pre-colonial education enabled people to sustain their livelihoods and steer development in their respective communities. This should not be interpreted to mean that crisis was unheard of in pre-colonial period. People experienced different kinds of crises, but the crises were dealt with accordingly and through innovative thinking and the use of available [indigenous] knowledges. The environmental crisis that the people experienced, for example, was responded to with dismal failure at times, and resounding success at others, as the trial and error methods were seen to be effective (see also O'Donoghue *et al.*, 1999). As the adage "necessity is the mother of invention" goes, these crises were springboards of innovative thinking. Through trial and error, people could try this and that IK and sometimes come up with new knowledge that successfully combated or reduced the gravity of the crisis. For this reason, scholars like Ntuli (1999: 189) argue that "the role of higher education and that of intellectuals generally, in shaping the direction towards a more culture specific or culturally relevant curriculum, is a critical one". The same argument is echoed by Vilakazi (1999: 206, emphasis original) who warns that "Africa needs to formulate *and implement well thought out* policies which would result in initiating an agricultural revolution, to be able to feed her millions of people adequately and lay a basis for education, industrialisation and modernisation". Though Vilakazi's argument is side with IKs especially in the area of agriculture, it is critical in that it emphasises the importance of integrating IKs in education systems in Africa.

While integrating indigenous knowledge into the mainstream education curriculum is worthwhile for any country in Africa, this should not end there: a lot more should follow. This should include continuous monitoring and evaluation/assessment of the curriculum by stakeholders and educational technocrats so as to keep up and enhance the relevancy, significance, and quality of education being offered. This is critical as curriculum is just like a garden that requires constant care-taking to ensure that it keeps on flourishing. The importance of education curriculum evaluation has been underscored by Lotz, Tselane and Wagiet (1998) who have argued that assessment of education curriculum should be a continuous process of gathering evidence of learning throughout the school life of a learner in order to be able to determine the quality, impact, and value of the learning process and programme as a whole.

Indigenous knowledge (IK) in Africa: Institutionalisation and integration in education curricular

In the recent years, there has been realisation of the importance of institutionalising and integrating indigenous knowledge into the mainstream education curricula across the African continent. To this effect, some strides have been made by African governments to make sure that IKs are institutionalised and integrated into the mainstream education curricula. However, a few African countries have so far established IK institutions in their countries, worse still integrating indigenous knowledge into the mainstream education curriculum. Examples of institutions that have been created on the continent in an attempt to promote IKs include South African Resource Centre for Indigenous Knowledge (SARCIK) (South Africa), Cameroon Indigenous Knowledge Organisation (CIKO) (Cameroon), Association for the Promotion of Indigenous Knowledge (APIC) (Ethiopia), Nigerian Centre for Indigenous Knowledge (NIRCIK) (Nigeria), Centre Burkinabè de Recherche sur les Pratiques et Savoirs Paysans (BURCIK)(Burkina Faso), Kenya Resource Centre for Indigenous Knowledge (KENRIK) (Kenya), Ghana Resource Centre for Indigenous Knowledge (GhaRCIK)(Ghana), Masailand Resource Centre for Indigenous Knowledge (MARECIK)(Tanzania), Madagascar Resource Centre for Indigenous Knowledge (MARCIK) (Madagascar), and Zimbabwe Resource Centre for Indigenous Knowledge (ZIRCIK) (Zimbabwe). At regional level, there is the African Resource Centre for Indigenous Knowledge (ARCIK) which is an institution representing the African continent as a whole.

Yet the fact remains that while there has been a realisation of the importance of IKs in Africa, a lot more is still desired to be done across the whole continent to ensure that IKs are fully institutionalised and integrated in education curricular not only at tertiary level, but also at primary and secondary levels. Many African countries still lag behind in institutionalising IKs and integrating them in their education curricula: the Western based curricula thus continue dominating many education systems on the continent and in the name of globalisation. This is in spite of the fact that globalisation itself has been criticised by many scholars (see for example Ngugi 1986; Shizha 2010; Mawere 2012; Nicolaides 2012) as a threat to non-Western cultures and indigenous knowledges. Writing about the spreading of Euro-American ideas across Africa in the guise of globalisation, Nicolaides (2012: 118) laments:

> *American norms, values and practices are being conveyed across the Atlantic as the suitable mode of behaviour for Africans. As a consequence of this cultural migration, Africa's rich culture is being degraded and is viewed as inferior by many Africans.*

In one of my poems, Mawere (2013: 3-4) I also lament moral decadence in youths as a result of the tide of westernisation and globalisation that has swept across Africa:

> *Our hearts*
> *Elders*
> *Are heavy*
> *Replete with much sorrow*
> *Caught on prevaricated crossroads*
> *Penetrating deep the labyrinth of the hearts of our youths*

The leaders of the day tomorrow
We see only sluiced conscience build around crucibles of mist
smoke
Their minds
Chartered with the vertigo of westernisation
That our forefathers condemned in their loud voices
Never would they dare imagining chasing the western ghettos of
the day
And these odd cultures writhed in manacles of globalisation
Harbingers of bad omen on the land...
The night now never fall
Flowering girls never sleep even a minute
Following the seditious rays of the new sun that never sets
Only to be stubbornly harvested raw
Shattering hard the dreams of their forefathers...

This lamentation echoes Ladislaus Semali's (1999: 97-98) critical observation of the early years of Tanzania's post-independence education:

While teaching in Tanzania in the early years of the post-independence era, I struggled like many teachers in African schools to develop relevant and meaningful lessons which met the local needs of students, drawing on examples of the history and wisdom of local people, parents, and grandparents. Unfortunately, many of the examples I used in Tanzanian classrooms were not found in textbooks available at the time. We read, for example, Shakespeare,.....Greek mythologies, and the famous Arabian stories of Alfu-Lela-Ulela and Ali Baba and his seven sons. Missing in these works were examples of local imagery, history, folklore, and African beliefs. Instead, students were taught to value and admire the beliefs, stories, histories, and myths of other nations...Indigenous knowledge was the unofficial knowledge......

Similarly, the Kenyan renowned Eurocentric critic, Ngugi wa Thiongo's (1986) argues that postcolonial education in Africa is full of inadequacies and cultural shocks with Western biased content and practices, most of which corrupt the minds of all those experience it. Wa Thiongo (1986: 7) thus observes:

Colonial education was far from giving people the confidence in their ability and capacities to overcome obstacles or to become masters of the laws governing external nature as human beings and tends to make them feel their inadequacies and their inability to do anything about the conditions of their lives.

From the foregoing, it can be safely argued that the content and practices in these Western biased education systems (which in fact was inherited from the former colonial system of education) have always alienated African students such that most of them (African students) were brainwashed to the extent that they fail to solve their daily problems, and worse still, like their former colonial maters continue despising their own [African] culture and people: the Western biased education undermines African indigenous knowledge and compromises the learning process of the African students. This implies that even today, many Africans across the continent are still mentally colonised yet it was expected of African governments that immediate after independence they decolonise their education curricula through integration of indigenous knowledges and refocus of pedagogy on African perspectives so as to help expedite decolonisation of

132

the African mind. Wa Thiongo, thus, calls for the decolonisation of not only the minds of the African people who experience Western education, but also of the education systems that Africa inherited from Europe and continue passing it on to posterity. Such critical observations as Wa Thiongo's warrant urgent need for each and every African country to revisit its educational curriculum and carefully align it with both the immediate and long term needs of the continent based on the African people's aspirations, creativity, and available resources in the people's disposal. This transformative, progressive and pragmatic approach to contemporary education management and planning is critical in addressing the long standing disparities in the utilisation of knowledge that is African versus knowledge that is Western oriented. This is simply because all forms of knowledge (whether indigenous, African, Western or Eastern) is spawned within a particular segment of society based on power and class (Gergen 2001:126). No wonder why the adage "knowledge is power" is so popular across the world. Having reached the same conclusion in their analysis of the dynamics of knowledge and power, Aronowitz and Giroux (1985:81) support the view that certain segments of society popularise what is to be considered as knowledge when they argue that "schools play a particularly important role in legitimising and producing dominant cultural capital through the hierarchically arranged bodies of school knowledge". This implies that in Africa, where Western-based/former colonial education systems continue existing in many schools across the continent, the consequence is the perpetuation of an education that is irrelevant to the African context. Sifuna and Sawamura (2008) give an excellent example of such a scenario whereby in the 1960s, the Education Development Centre

(EDC) of Newton Massachusetts was launched as the 'African Education Programme', when it was only meant for the Anglophone countries. Under this project, the EDC initiated the African Mathematics Programme (AMP), the African Primary Science Programme (APSP) and the African Social Science Programme (ASSP) in the 'false' name of curriculum reforms. It later on turned out that this project was never a real and helpful curriculum reform as the programmes had no direct relevance to the African context and worse still to the indigenous programmes decolonised states in Africa required. Such reprocessing or salvaging of colonial models of education is a result of gullibility on the part of African governments as well as lack of well-defined framework. This is also because most of the African states even after independence in the 1960s and 1980s continued to use the systems (political, educational, economic and so on) they inherited from their former colonisers. There is need, therefore, for African states to have a clear vision and framework in all their national institutions including education, and to stop instantly from relying on colonial or Western models in solving African problems except in those instances where use of the models is deemed completely necessary.

Granted, the continued use of Western models means that certain forms of knowledge, particularly the hegemonic Western forms, might continue to be accorded lofty status in the education curricula across the world at the detriment of knowledge forms from other continents like Africa. It is no doubt that such one – sided curricula, which in fact are existent in many African societies, require urgent careful revision: the curricula require serious deconstruction and reconstruction so as to stop disadvantaging learners from formerly marginalised (or colonised) societies such as those of Africa. As argued by Outlaw (1987: 11), to deconstruct colonial school curricula is "to displace them into the fabric of historicity out of which they have been shaped: it is to become involved in the unmaking of a construct" and restoring humanity of the de-humanised Africans. On the basis of this argument, deconstruction and reconstruction in African education curricula throughout the continent would entail a complete rebut of the hegemonic structures of Euro-American defined epistemology: even the conceptualisation of some concepts such as illiterate as understood from the Western perspective would need rigorous and careful revision. This is because in many African societies, many rural people are considered illiterate by Western standards, yet they have particular areas [areas of specialisation] they know better than those [intellectuals] who label them as such. Alluding to the same point Ntuli (1999: 197) argues that "a number of intellectuals and academics consult traditional healers whom it is assumed that they are illiterate according to western standards. If these academics and intellectuals had possessed the traditional knowledge of healing, it would be unnecessary to consult traditional healers". Also, there are many people in the African rural communities who have never attended any Western-based educational institution, who cannot read and write, but can tell stories [as story tellers] much better than those that we read from books. A million dollar question can therefore be raised here: "Who is more literate (in terms of story-telling), the rural village folk and the story-teller we encounter in the books?" The answer is evident. This means that most of the concepts that Africa adopted or that were imposed on Africa by the West are in many cases rendered inapplicable and useless by African standards, that is, when

135

they are approached from an African perspective. In such instances, local definitions inspired by the African cultural milieu should be used to replace the old concepts adopted from the West or at least to critically redefine them; otherwise one would be justified to argue that Western concepts are local (and not universal) as has been done with the concept of indigenous knowledge by Eurocentric scholars.

The other thing that might be important in the institutionalisation and integration of indigenous knowledge in Africa is to make sure that in higher education (universities and colleges), IKs are not only studied in particular areas of study. As the situation stands right now in many African countries where attempts are being made to institutionalise and integrate indigenous knowledge into tertiary education, IKs are mainly offered in the areas of Arts and Cultural studies. In many Southern African and Zimbabwean institutions of higher education, for example, the general assumption currently held is that indigenous knowledges are an integral part of the Arts and Culture Learning Area. As such, in many African universities where indigenous knowledge is offered as a degree programme, it has been aligned to the Culture Learning Area. In view of this observation, I argue that such a strategy though positive in that it is an important stride towards the recognition of the value of IKs, it still marginalises indigenous knowledge. My sense is that indigenous knowledge systems should be taught across all disciplines whether social sciences, natural sciences, or arts and culture so as to give voice to all Africans in whatever area of study (or specialisation) they happen to be. In social sciences such as environmental studies, for example, indigenous knowledges related to agriculture and conservation could be taught. In natural sciences, indigenous knowledges to do with mathematics, biology and so on could also be taught. And, in the arts and culture area, indigenous knowledge to do with children's traditional games, basketry, curving and so on could also be offered. I should underscore, however, that in order to do this, there is need for careful curriculum planning, designing and implementation to ensure that careful and appropriate integration of indigenous knowledge is done.

It may also be of utmost importance to ensure that indigenous knowledges (as currently with Western science in many African schools) are taught right across all levels of education not only in tertiary institutions such as universities and colleges. This would ensure that children are taught the value and importance of their indigenous knowledge systems when they are still young. Otherwise Rodney's (1982) observation that the educated Africans are the most alienated of all Africans will persist as long as we continue using Western-based education curricula in African learning institutions. As Rodney (1982: 275) himself observed of the impact of Western oriented education on Africans:

> *The educated Africans were the most alienated Africans on the continent. At each further stage of education, they were battered and succumbed to the white capitalist, and after being given salaries, they could then afford to sustain a style of life imported from outside...That further transformed their mentality.*

Rodney's observation echoes Julius Nyerere (1968: 278), the first president of Tanzania's lamentation in view of the African child educated in Western oriented schools:

At present our pupils learn to despise even their own parents because they are old-fashioned and ignorant; there is nothing in our existing educational system which suggests to the pupil that he [she] can learn important things about farming from his [her] elders. The result is that he [she] absorbs beliefs about witchcraft before he [she] goes to school; but does not learn the properties of local grasses; he [she] absorbs taboos from his family but does not learn the methods of making nutritious traditional foods. And from school, he [she] acquires knowledge unrelated to agricultural life. He [she] gets the worst of both systems!

Researching with Francophone Africa, Holsinger and Cowell (2000) also made a somehow similar observation as Rodney and Nyerere's. They observed that foreign knowledge was borrowed from France and in most if not all cases with little or no involvement of the local or regional players, for example, education stakeholders. As Holsinger and Cowell further noted, this impacted negatively on the consumers of that knowledge who in most cases were the youth. It is in this sense that I argue IK should be taught right from the Primary School level through Secondary School level to tertiary levels. IKs, thus, should be integrated as valuable systems of knowledge in education policies at all levels. This would help to guarantee an education system that fosters a process of learning that is liberating and based on the incorporation of indigenous capital content. Once this is done, it becomes much easier for students to develop innovative thinking, thinking that is prepared to make use of resource at hand for self-sustenance and community development. This is critical because indigenous knowledge systems of any culture (whether African or Western) are embedded in the cultural and historical environments of the people or society in question. Failure to do this has proven to be disastrous in Africa as development in many countries continues to stagger, moral indecency play havoc in destroying the notion of family and societal fabric, and environmental degradation among other problems becomes even more complex than ever. This thinking is in accord with the *South African White Paper on Education and Training* (1995:22) which clearly states that all programmes of education and training should "encourage independent and critical thought, the capacity to question, enquire, reason, weigh evidence and form judgements, achieve understanding, recognise the provisional and incomplete nature of most human knowledge". Integrating indigenous knowledge in education at all levels (primary, secondary and tertiary), thus, is likely to enhance sustainable development in Africa.

Integrating indigenous knowledge in Africa's formal education system: Potential for enhancing sustainable development

The value and fundamental importance of indigenous knowledge can only be easily recognised and appreciated in today's communities (both rural and urban communities) if they are mainstreamed or integrated into education systems and development processes. This is because processes of science that include rational observation of natural events, classification, and problem solving are woven into all aspects of indigenous cultures (Snively and Corsiglia 2001) for they help students or children in general to develop and shape their own social and cultural identities as a people. As such,

Students who are exposed to this knowledge are capable of making sense of their lives and develop a cultural identity that mirrors their social and cultural communities. African science education has been criticised for its lack of relevance to African cultures, being a collection of facts from 'western' science with little or no adaptation and less critical, and fact-transmission oriented pedagogy (Shizha 2010: 28).

As pointed out by World Bank (1998: 31), awareness creation, pilot applications, and mainstreaming are the three elements required for a successful integration of IK into the development process. These tripartite elements suggest that the first step towards recognition and integration of indigenous knowledge in education and development projects requires a careful focus on awareness building among stakeholders and decision-makers in education, development organisations and the national governments. At the second level, such awareness would help to develop pilots, that is, careful selection of projects, communities or countries where IKs are being used successfully so as to convince other colleagues and partners. This would help to publicise and emphasise the importance of indigenous knowledge cases across communities through exhibitions or presentations during partner events such as meetings and conferences. Once this is done, the later stage would shift to mainstreaming through integration into the education systems and development projects. This could be understood to be implementation level where policy makers realise the need to put issues of indigenous knowledge in policy documents. This stage, thus, would take into cognisance the use of 'success stories' as a way of demonstrating that indigenous knowledge can bring value to education and development in communities.

An analysis of these tripartite elements enunciated by the World Bank, however, shows that creating awareness, pilot applications and mainstreaming alone are not adequate to foster sustainable development especially in rural communities where these indigenous knowledges are produced. There is need to acknowledge and put on board the people where the indigenous knowledges in question are produced so that no resistance will be faced at implementation and monitoring levels; otherwise local communities will resist any move towards the exploitation of their indigenous knowledge in whatever way except if they are actively involved. The analysis I am making here resonates with Flavier *et al*'s advice to development agencies. Warning developing agencies on issues to do with addressing the problems of environment, Flavier *et al* (1999: 482) says: "Go to the people, live among the people, learn from the people, plan with the people, work with the people, start with what the people know, build on what the people have, teach by showing, and learn by doing". Flavier *et al*'s advice here is worth considering as it is only when community members feel that their views, norms and values are seriously considered, and when they [community members] feel they are being treated as equal partners (who can teach as well as learn) that they can support development projects initiated by external agencies. Now given that most of the rural people are 'uncertificated' (in terms of Western education standards), their contribution can largely come through offering indigenous knowledge to external development experts while they are also learning from them [the experts].

Yet more often than not, education policy makers and development agencies/experts ask themselves: "What can we learn from illiterate people?" This is because for them, being literate entails having been educated in Western institutions or using Western-biased models in development interventions. I argue that this is a narrow conception of literacy, and that literacy should encompass other elements from societies other than the Western ones. In fact Western standards should not be used as the sole measure for determining literacy: such politics around issues of knowledge production and advancement should be abandoned. Granted, local communities no matter how low their education level (by Western standards) is, they always have their knowledge that has to be considered as distinct and valuable. Chatterjee (2004: 66) alludes to the same point when he argues that government agencies "have to descend from [the] high ground to the terrain of the political society in order to renew their legitimacy as providers of wellbeing". This is critical because it is problematic for development agencies to remain in absolute control of community development given that it is through this [indigenous] knowledge that indigenous people, well before their contact with Europeans, always used to relate with the world. Indigenous knowledge, thus, has to be seriously considered to ensure the wellbeing of people it is meant to serve – those in the rural communities across the continent. In many African societies, for example, children from young ages are taught through practice, folktales, taboos, and rituals that forests are an important part of human life that serves as a source of food and medicine, used as building materials and places of worship, among others. Emphasising the latter (forests as places for worship), Kipury (1983) observes in indigenous Kenyan communities (e.g.

142

Agĩkũyũ) that many people believed that forests were the manifestation of the power of the Supreme Being [God] such that big trees like fig trees and baobabs were set apart as shrines/places of worship. Recent studies carried out by Kabira and Mutahi (1993) among the Agĩkũyũ communities of Kenya also revealed that even in the present day Kenya, it is a taboo to cut a *mũgumo* (fig tree) in this community because it is still regarded as sacred – a place where people can worship God. Such beliefs are also common among some rural communities of Zimbabwe and Mozambique where big trees such as baobab and mahogany are used as *marombo*, that is, places to petition rain from God through the ancestors. Rain petitioning ceremonies (*mukwerere*) was done (and is still done in some places) under those trees when rain season approaches. Yet this should not be misinterpreted to mean that Africans across the continent animate. They don't animate but respect their environment. Respect for the environment (environment conservation) was also a common thing that every child could learn as s/he grew up in Maasai communities of Kenya and Tanzania (Kipury 1983) as with many other children across the continent. As further noted by Kipury, among the Maasai, trees and shrubs are respected because they provide shade for various social gatherings. Furthermore, the Maasai people being pastoralists, they highly value grass and trees as a blessing from God for their animals. They also use trees for certain purification rituals. Chesaina (1997: 40) aptly captures the importance of the *nharaunda* (surroundings) or the universe to human beings:

> *Oral literary works are intricately related to the social environment of the people who create and perform them … the universe is a complex phenomenon and human beings need to*

understand it in order to build a niche for themselves in it. Oral literature helps people to understand the natural environment and their place within the environment.

All these values were embedded in the indigenous knowledge systems of the different cultures across Africa. This entails that indigenous knowledge systems were an equivalent of the Western education curriculum in African schools today. Yet in many education curricula across the African continent, indigenous knowledges have not been taken aboard despite the acknowledgement by many policy makers and curriculum scholars on Africa that the place of the learner and his/her culture are central in the learning process of children. As previously highlighted, indigenous knowledges and other such cultural values were communicated mainly through oral literature. Asenath Odaga (1984: 9) confirms this when she observes that "oral literature acts as a vehicle of communication, conveying cultural values, wisdom, philosophy, history, knowledge and skills". The value of this indigenous curriculum, important as it was, cannot be underestimated: modern day education can draw important insights and improve its curriculum by integrating these forms of knowledge [IKSs] into the mainstream education system.

Notes

1. United Nations Conference on Environment and Development (UNCED). 1992. *United Nations Conference* (June 1992), Rio de Janeiro, Brazil.

2. International Development Research Centre of Canada (IDRC). 1992. *International Conference on "Indigenous Knowledge and Sustainable Development"* (September 1992), Silang, Philippines.

3. Davies, S. and Ebbe, K. 1995. (Eds). *Traditional knowledge and sustainable development: Proceedings of a conference*, held at the World Bank in September 1993, World Bank, Environmentally sustainable development proceedings Series No. 4, Washington D.C.

4. James D. Wolfensohn, 1998. *Address to the 1998 Annual Meetings of the World Bank and the IMF*, Washington: USA.

5. Mignolo, W. 2000. *Local histories/Global designs: Essays on the coloniality of power, subaltern knowledges and border thinking*, Princeton University Press: Princeton.

6. Grosfoguel, R. 2006. World-System analysis in the context of transmodernity, border thinking and global coloniality, *Review 29*.

Bibliography

Achebe, C. 1958. *Things fall apart,* Heinemann: United Kingdom.

Adams, J. L. 1991. *Flying buttresses, entropy, and o-rings: The world of an engineer,* MA: Harvard University Press.

Agrawal, A. 1995a. Indigenous and Scientific Knowledge: Some Critical Comments, *Indigenous Knowledge and Development Monitor,* 3 (3): 3-6.

Agrawal, A. 1995b. Dismantling the divide between indigenous knowledge and scientific knowledge, *Development and Change,* 26 (3): 413-439.

Altieri, M.A. 1995. *Agro-ecology: The Science of Sustainable Agriculture,* 2nd Edition, London: IT Publications.

Aronowitz, S. & Giroux, H. A. 1985. *Education under siege: The conservative, liberal and radical debate over schooling,* Routledge & Kegan: London.

Association for the Promotion of Indigenous Knowledge (APIK), Addis Ababa University, Ethiopia.

Bastian, A. (Ed). 2009. Encyclopaedia Britannica, (27/01/09). Available   at: http://www.britanica.com/EBchecked/topics/55606/Adolf-Bastian.

Battiste, M. 2002. *Indigenous Knowledge and Pedagogy in First Nations Education: A Literature Review with Recommendations*, Ottawa: Apamuwek Institute.

Benedict, E.T. 1959. *An anthropologist at work: Writings of Ruth Benedict*, Boston, MA: Houghton Mifflin.

Bhebe, N. 2000. *The Zapu and Zanu guerrilla warfare and the evangelical Lutheran Church in Zimbabwe,* Studia Missionalia Upsaliensia.

Bhola, H. S. 2002. Reclaiming Old Heritage for Proclaiming Future History: The Knowledge for Development Debate in African Contexts, *Africa Today*, 49 (3): 3-21.

Biko, S. 1978. *I write what I like* (edited by Alreaed Stubbs), Heinmann, London.

Bijker, W., Hughes, T. P., & Pinch, T. 1987. General introduction, In Bijker, W., Hughes, T. P., & T. Pinch, T. (Eds), *The social construction of technological systems: New directions in the sociology and history of technology*, MA: MIT Press: Cambridge.

Blaikie, P., Brown, K., Stocking, M., Tang, L., Dixon, P., & Sillitoe, P. 1997. Knowledge in action: Local knowledge as a development resource and barriers to its incorporation in natural resource research and development, *Agricultural Systems* 55, pp. 217-37.

Blakeney, M. 1997. Bioprospecting and the Protection of Traditional Medical Knowledge of Indigenous Peoples:

An Australian Perspective, *European Intellectual Property Review*, Vol. 19 (6): 298-303.

Blakeney, M. 1999. Intellectual property in the dreamtime – protecting the cultural creativity of indigenous peoples, WP 11/99, *OIPRC Electronic Journal of Intellectual Property Rights*, www.oiprc. ox.ac.uk/EJWP1199.html (accessed 12 September 2013).

Boaventura de Sousa, S. 2007. (Ed). *Cognitive justice in global world: Prudent knowledge for a decent life*, Lanham: Lexington.

Bodeker, G. & Kronenberg, F. 2002. A Public Health Agenda for Complementary, Alternative and Traditional (indigenous) Medicine, *American Journal of Public Health*, 2 (10): 1582-1591.

Burkitt, I. 2002. Technologies of the self: *Habitus* and capacities, *Journal for the Theory of Social Behaviour, 32* (2): 219-237.

Cameroon Indigenous Knowledge Organisation (CIKO), Yaounde, Cameroon.

Cassie, Q. 2009. Globalisation and science Education: The implications for indigenous Knowledge systems, *International Education Studies*, 2 (1): 76-89.

Caxton, M. 2002. Cited In Eade, D. (Ed). 2002. *Culture and Development*, Oxfam GB: Oxford.

Chavunduka, G. L. 1982. *Witches, witchcraft and the Law in Zimbabwe, Occasional Paper No. 1 (1982)*, ZINATHA: Harare.

Chavunduka, G.1994. *African Traditional Medicine,* Harare: UZ Publications, Zimbabwe.

Chavunduka, G. 1980. Witchcraft and the law in Zimbabwe, *Zambezia Journal of the University of Zimbabwe,* (1980): VIII, 129-47.

Chatterjee, P. 2004. *The politics of the governed,* Columbia University Press: New York, USA.

Chesaina, C. 1997. *Oral Literature of the Embu and Mbeere,* East African Publishers: Nairobi, Kenya.

Compton, V. 2004. *The relationship between science and technology: discussion document prepared for the New Zealand Ministry of Education Curriculum Project,* New Zealand.

Compton, V. and France, B. 2007. Redefining technological literacy in New Zealand: from concepts to curriculum constructs, In Dakers, J. R., Dow, W. J., & De Vries, M. J. (Eds). 2007. *Teaching and Learning Technological Literacy in the Classroom,* Proceedings of the PATT-18 International Conference on Design and Technology Educational Research (pp. 260 - 272). Glasgow: University of Glasgow.

Das Gupta, A. 2011. Does indigenous knowledge have anything to deal with sustainable development? *Antrocom Online Journal of Anthropology*, 7(1): 57-64.

Davies, S.et al. 2009. Discussing dialogue: perspectives on the value of science dialogue events that do not inform policy, *Public Understanding of Science, 18* (3): 338–353.

De Beer, J. and Whitlock, E. 2009. Indigenous Knowledge in the Life Sciences Classroom: Put on your de Bono Hats!, *American Biology Teacher*, 71 (4): 209-216.

Dei, J. S. 2002. African development: The relevance and implications of indigenousness, In Dei, J. S., Budd, H., and Rosenberg, G. (Eds). 2002. *Indigenous knowledge in global contexts: Multiple readings of our world*, University of Toronto Press: Toronto, pp.1-17.

De Walt, B. 1994. Using Indigenous Knowledge to Improve Agriculture and Natural Resource Management, *Human Organisation*, 53 (2): 123 – 131.

Duri, F. and Mapara. J. 2007. Environmental Awareness and Management in Pre-colonial Zimbabwe, *Zimbabwe Journal of Geographical Research,* Volume 1 (2): 98-111.

Economist Intelligence Unit (1985–1998), Redhouse Press, London.

Elgin, C. Z. 2004. True enough. In Sosa, E. & Villanueva, E. (Eds). *Epistemology* (pp. 113–131), Blackwell Publishers: Boston.

Ellen, R. and Harris, H. 1996. Concepts of indigenous environmental knowledge in scientific and development studies literature – A critical assessment; draft paper East-West Environmental Linkages Network Workshop 3, Canterbury.

Fairhead, J. and Leach, M. 1995. False Forest History, Complicit Social Analysis: Rethinking some West African Environmental Narratives, *World development*, 23 (6): 1023-1035.

Fanon, F. 1967. *Black skin, white masks* (translated by Charles, L. Markmann), Grove Press: New York, USA.

Fanon, F. 1968. *The wretched of the earth* (translated by Richard Philcox), Grove Press: New York, USA.

Feenberg, A. 2006. What is philosophy of technology? In Dakers, J. (Ed). 2006. *Defining technological literacy: Towards an epistemological framework*, pp. 5-16, Palgrave Macmillan: New York.

Fellows, R. 1995. Introduction, In R. Fellows (Ed), *Philosophy and technology*, Cambridge University Press: Cambridge.

Flavier, J. M. et al. 1995. 'The regional programme for the promotion of indigenous knowledge in Asia', pp. 479-487, In Warren, D.M., L.J. Slikkerveer and D. Brokensha (eds) The cultural dimension of development: Indigenous knowledge systems. London: Intermediate Technology Publications.

Flavier, J. M., De Jesus, A., & Mavarro, S. 1999. Regional program for the promotion of Indigenous Knowledge in Asia, In Warren, D. M., Slikkerveer, L. J., & Brokensha, D. (Eds). *The cultural dimension of development: Indigenous Knowledge Systems*, SRP, Exeter: London.

Fofana, S. Y. et al. 1993. Etude relative au feu aup& des populations des bassins versants types du Haut Niger: Monographies des Bassins Kan I, Kan II, Kiss II. *Report Conakry: Rtpublique de GuinCe*: Programme d' Amtnagement des Bassins Versants Haut-Niger.

Foucault, M. 1988. Technologies of the self, In Martin, L. H., Gutman, H., & Hutton, P. H. 1988. (Eds.), *Technologies of the self: A seminar with Michel Foucault*, pp. 16-49. Cambridge, MA: MIT Press.

Galtung, J. 1970. *Development: The post-revolutionary perspective,* Bulletin of Peace Proposals, 1 (1970): 375-380.

Gardner, P. 1994. The relationship between technology and science, *International Journal of Technology and Design Education, 4*, 123-153.

Garlake, P. 1982a. *Life at Great Zimbabwe,* Gweru: Mambo Press, Zimbabwe.

Garlake, P. 1982b. *Great Zimbabwe described and explained*, Zimbabwe Publishing House: Harare, Zimbabwe.

Garlake, P. 1992. *People making history*, Zimbabwe Publishing House, Harare: Zimbabwe.

153

Gergen, K. J. 2001. *Social construction in context*, Sage Publishers: London.

Gibson, N. 2011. *Fanonian practices in South Africa: From Steve Biko to Abahlali baseMjondolo,* University of Kwa-Zulu Natal Press, South Africa.

Gelfand, M. 1979. *Growing Up in Shona Society*, Mambo Press: Gweru, Zimbabwe.

Goduka, I 2000. Indigenous ways of knowing: Affirming a legacy, pp. 134-145, In E.M Chiwome, et. al (Eds). *Indigenous Knowledge and Technology in African and Diasporan Communities: Multi-Disciplinary Approaches*, Southern African Association for Culture and Development: Harare, Zimbabwe.

Green, E. C. 1996. Indigenous knowledge systems and health promotion in Mozambique, In Normann, H., Snyman, I., & Cohen, M., (Eds). *Indigenous knowledge and its use*, SRP, Exeter: London.

Green, L. Unpublished manuscript. Beyond South Africa's IK-Science wars: On knowledges and ways of knowing in postcolonial universities, *University of Cape Town, South Africa.*

Green, L. 2008. 'Indigenous knowledge' and 'science': Reframing the debate on knowledge diversity. *Archaeologies*, 4 (1): 144–163.

Green, L. 2009. Challenging epistemologies: exploring knowledge practices in Palikur astronomy. *Futures* 41 (1): 41-52.

Grosfoguel, R. 2006. World-System analysis in the context of transmodernity, border thinking and global coloniality, *Review 29.*

Hagmann J. et al. 1996. In Reij C. et al. (Eds.), *Sustaining the soil: Indigenous soil and water conservation in Africa*, Earthscan.

Hall, E.T. 1992. *The Hidden Dimension*, New York, Anchor Books.

Harvey, T. E. C. 1962. A short account of correlated popular herbal remedies of the Nyanga of Matabeleland, *Central African Journal of Medicine,* 8 (1962): 305-310.

Holsinger, D. B. and Cowell, R.N. 2000. *Positioning secondary school education in developing countries: Expansion and curriculum,* UNESCO: IIEP Publications.

Horsthemke, K. 2008. The idea of indigenous knowledge, *Archaeologies: Journal of the World Archaeological Congress,* 4(1): 129–143.

Horsthemke, K. 2010. Diverse epistemologies, truth and archaeology: In defence of realism, *Science and engineering ethics.* Published online @DOI: 10.1007/s11948-009-9194-6.

Hountondji, P. 1997. (Ed). *Endogenous knowledge: Research trails,* CODESRIA, Senegal.

Hoyos, C. 2000. 'Staying cool naturally', *Financial Times,* Monday October 9, 2000.

http://www.sedac.ciesin.columbia.edu website

Huffman, T. N. 1971. The possible prehistory of the proposed Hunyani Dam – The iron age, *Journal of the Prehistory of Rhodesia,* Number 7, July 1971.

Human Development Report. 1996. Growth for human development: Overview, *United Nations Development Programme,* New York: USA.

Ikuenobe, P. 1999. Moral thought in African cultures: A metaphysical question, *African Philosophy,* Vol.12, No.2, August.

International Technology Education Association. 2002. (2nd ed). *Standards for technological literacy: content for the study of technology,* VA: ITEA, Reston.

Ishemo, S. L. 2002. Culture, liberation, and 'development,' In Eade, D. (Ed.). 2002. *Development and culture: Selected essays from development in practice,* (pp. 25-37), Oxfam GB: Oxford in association with World Faiths Development Dialogue.

Jackson, J. G. 1970. *Introduction to African civilisations,* Kensington Publishing Corporation: New York.

Kabira, W. and Mutahi, K. 1993. *Gikuyu oral literature*, East African Publishers: Nairobi, Kenya.

Kargbo, J. A. 2005. Managing Indigenous Knowledge: What Is The Role For Public Libraries In Sierra Leone? *The International Information and Library Review* 37.

Kawooya, D. 2006. Indigenous Knowledge and Africa's University Libraries: The Case of Uganda, *World Library and Information Congress: 72nd IFLA General Conference and Council.* 20-24 August 2006, Seoul, Korea. Available online @ http://www.ifla.org/iv/ifla72/index.htm.

Kipury, N. 1983. *Oral Literature of the Maasai*, East African Publishers: Nairobi, Kenya.

Kotze, D. A. 1984. *Development policies and approaches in Southern Africa*, Academica Press: Pretoria, South Africa.

Kluckhohn, F. R. & Strodtbeck, F. L. 1961. *Variations in value orientations*, Evanston, IL: Row, Peterson.

Kunnie, J. 2005. Decolonising the University: Utilising an indigenous cultural framework to develop curricula in education to transform the African continental context, *Paper presented to The South African Society For Research and Development in Higher Education (SAARDHE) Conference*, University of KwaZulu-Natal, 26-29 June 2005.

Lacan, J. 1964. *The four fundamental concepts of psychoanalysis*, Hogarth Press, London.

Latour, B. 1993. *We have never been modern,* Cambridge, Mass: Harvard University Press.

Latour, B. 2007. The recall of modernity, *Cultural Studies Review* 13 (1): 11-30.

Lawson, C. 2008. An ontology of technology: Artefacts, relations and functions, *Technè, 12* (1): 48-64.

Lotz, H., Tselane, T., & Wagiet, R. 1998. *Supporting curriculum 2005,* Government Printer, Pretoria: South Africa.

Maila, M. W. 2001. The assessment of learning programmes for the Senior Phase at Environmental Education Centres in Mpumalanga, *Unpublished M Ed thesis,* University of South Africa: Pretoria.

Maila, M. W. and Loubser, C. P. 2003. Emancipatory indigenous knowledge systems: Implications for environmental education in South Africa, *South African Journal of Education,* 23 (4): 276-280.

Mapara, J. 2009. Indigenous Knowledge Systems in Zimbabwe: Juxtaposing Postcolonial Theory, *Journal of Pan African Studies,* 3 (1): 139-155.

Marchal, Y. J. 1986. Vingt ans de lutte antiérosive au nord du Burkina Faso, *Cahiers Orstom: Série Pédologie* XXII (2): 173-180.

Marx, K. 1859/1977. *A contribution to the critique of political economy,* Progress Publishers, Moscow.

Masailand Resource Centre for Indigenous Knowledge (MARECIK), Arusha, Tanzania.

Mawere, M. 2010. The Impact of Mass Media on the Posterity of African Cultures: A Mozambican Case Study, *Africana: Journal of Ideas on Africa and the African Diaspora,* 4 (2): 143-164.

Mawere, M. 2012. *The struggle of African indigenous knowledge systems in an age of globalisation – A case for children's traditional games in South-eastern Zimbabwe,* Langaa RPCIG Publishers: Cameroon.

Mawere, M. 2013. *Lyrics of reason and experience,* Langaa RPCIG Publishers: Cameroon.

Mawere, M. 2011. *African belief and knowledge systems: A critical perspective,* Langaa RPCIG Publishers: Cameroon.

Mawere, M. And Kadenge, M. 2010. *Zvierwa* as African Indigenous Knowledge System: Epistemological and Ethical Implications of Selected Shona Taboos, *INDILA Journal of Africa Indigenous Knowledge,* 9 (1): 29-44.

Maweu, J. W. 2011. Indigenous ecological knowledge and modern western ecological knowledge: Complementary, not contradictory, *Thought and Practice: A Journal of the Philosophical Association of Kenya,* 3(2): 35-47.

Mazrui, A. 1993. Language and the quest for liberation in Africa: The legacy of Franz Fanon, *Third World Quarterly,* 14 (2): 348-365.

Mengara, D. M. 2001. (Ed). *Images of Africa: Stereotypes and Realities*, Africa World Press: Trenton and Asmara.

Mignolo, W. 2000. *Local histories/Global designs: Essays on the coloniality of power, subaltern knowledges and border thinking*, Princeton University Press: Princeton.

Misa, T. J. 2003. The compelling tangle of modernity and technology, In Misa, T. J., Brey, P., & Feenberg, A. (Eds), *Modernity and technology*, pp. 1-30, MA: The MIT Press: Cambridge.

Molefe Kete Asante, 2001. In Mengara, D. M. (Ed). 2001. *Images of Africa: Stereotypes and Realities,* Africa world Press: Trenton and Asmara.

Mondal, S. R. 2009. Biodiversity Management and Sustainable Development – The Issues of Indigenous Knowledge System and the Rights of Indigenous People with Particular Reference to North Eastern Himalayas of India, In Das Gupta, D. (Ed). 2009. *Indigenous Knowledge Systems and Common People's Rights*, Agrobios: Jodhpur, India.

Mudimbe, V. Y. 1988. *The Invention of Africa: Gnosis, Philosophy, and the Order of Knowledge*, Indiana University Press: Indiana.

Mwadime, K. N. R. 1999. Indigenous knowledge systems for an alternative culture in science: The role of nutritionists in Africa, In Semali L. M., & Kincheloe, J. L. (Eds).

(1999). *What is indigenous knowledge? Voices from the academy*, Falmer Press: New York.

Nakashima, D. J., Galloway-McLean, K., Thulstrup, H. D., Ramos-Castillo, A., and Rubis, J. T. 2012. *Weathering Uncertainty: Traditional knowledge for climate change assessment and adaptation,* Paris, UNESCO, and Darwin, UNU, pp. 120.

National Research Foundation (NRF) of South Africa, 2000. *Indigenous knowledge systems: Briefing,* 9 Feb 2000, Arts, Culture, Science and Technology Portfolio Committee, South Africa.

Nattrass, N. 2009. "Gender and Access to Antiretroviral Treatment in South Africa", *Feminist Economics,* 14 (4): 19-36.

Nicolaides, A. 2012. Globalization and Americanisation – The hijacking of indigenous African culture, *Global Advanced Research Journal of History, Political Science and International Relations,* 1 (6): 118-131.

Ntuli, P. 1999. The missing link between culture and education: Are we still chasing gods that are not our own? In: Makgoba, M. W. (Ed.). *African Renaissance,* Mafube – Tafelberg: Cape Town, South Africa.

Nyerere, J. 1968. Education for self-reliance, pp. 278-290. In Nyerere, J. 1968. (Ed). *Freedom and socialism/Uhuru na Ujamaa: Essays on socialism,* Oxford University Press.

Nyerere, J. K. 1968. Education for Self-reliance, In Nyerere J. K. (Ed). 1968. *Freedom and socialism: Uhuru na Ujamaa,* Dar es Salaam: Oxford University Press.

Nzewi, M. 2007. A Contemporary Study of Musical Arts: Informed by African Indigenous Knowledge Systems, *Volume Four Illuminations, Reflection and Explorations,* Ciima Series.

Obbo, C. 2006. 'But we know it all!' African perspectives on anthropological knowledge, In Ntarangwi, M., Mills, D., and Babiker, M., (Eds). 2006. *African anthropologies: History, critique and practice,* University of South Africa Press, South Africa.

Ocholla, D. 2007. Marginalized Knowledge: An Agenda for Indigenous Knowledge Development and Integration with Other Forms of Knowledge, *International Review of Information Ethics,* 7(09): 1-10.

Odaga, A. 1984. *Yesterday's Today: The Study of Oral Literature,* Lake Publishers and Enterprises: Kisumu.

O'Donoghue, R., Masuku, L., Janse van Rensburg, E., & Ward, M. 1999. Indigenous knowledge in/as Environmental Education processes, *EEASA Monograph,* No. 3. Share-Net: Howick.

Odora-Hoppers, C. 2001. *Indigenous knowledge and the integration of knowledge systems: Towards a conceptual and methodological Framework,* HSRC: Pretoria, South Africa.

Odora Hoppers, C. A. 2002. Introduction, In Odora Hoppers, C. A. (Ed). 2002. *Indigenous knowledge and the integration of knowledge systems*, pp. vii-xiv, Claremont: New Africa Books.

Outlaw, L. 1987. African 'philosophy': Deconstruction and reconstructive challenges, *Contemporary Philosophy: A New Survey* 5, 1-19.

Parlee, B. 2012. *Finding voice in a changing ecological and political landscape —Traditional knowledge and resource management in settled and unsettled claim areas of the Northwest Territories,* Canada, Aboriginal Policy Studies 2, pp. 56-87.

Prakash, N. P. 2013. Assessing the relevance of traditional knowledge for climate change adaptation in Rajasthan, *A Report Prepared for National Resources Management Programme,* New Delhi, India.

Project Kan II, 1992. Cited in Fairhead, J. and Leach, M. 1995. False Forest History, Complicit Social Analysis: Rethinking some West African Environmental Narratives, *World development,* 23 (6): 1023-1035.

Randles, W. G. L. 1979. (Translated by Roberts, R.S.) *The Empire of Monomatapa,* Gweru: Mambo Press, Zimbabwe.

Rodney, W. 1982. *How Europe underdeveloped Africa,* Harvard University Press: Washington DC, USA.

Sadomba W. Z. 1999. *In The Impact of Settler Colonisation on Indigenous Knowledge in Agriculture,* Wageningen.

Sapir, E. 1977. *Monograph series in language, culture and cognition*, Jupiter Press.

Saunders, R. 1996. *Economic Structural Adjustment Programme (ESAP)'s Fables 11*, Southern Africa Report, Vol. 11 (4), p.8, Zimbabwe.

Schein, E.H. 1992. *Organizational culture and leadership,* San Francisco: Jossey Bass.

Semali, L. M. 1999. Community as classroom: (Re)Valuing indigenous literacy, In Semali L. M., & Kincheloe, J. L. (Eds). 1999. *What is indigenous knowledge? Voices from the academy*, Falmer Press: New York.

Semali, L. M. & Kincheloe, J. L. 1999. Introduction: What is indigenous knowledge and why should we study it? In Semali L. M., & Kincheloe, J. L. (Eds). (1999). *What is indigenous knowledge? Voices from the academy*, Falmer Press: New York.

Sen, A. 1999. *Development as freedom*, Oxford University Press: London.

Shizha, E. 2010. The interface of neoliberal globalisation, science education and indigenous African knowledges in Africa, *Journal of Alternative Perspectives in the Social Sciences*, 2 (1): 27-58.

Shizha, E. 2013. Reclaiming our indigenous voices: The problem with postcolonial sub-Saharan African School curriculum, *Journal of Indigenous Social Development*, 2 (1): 1-18.

Sifuna, D. N. and Sawamura, N. 2008. Universalizing primary education in Kenya: Is it beneficial and sustainable? *Journal of International Cooperation in Education*, 11(3): 103-118.

Sillitoe, P. 1998. What know natives? Local knowledge in development, *Social Anthropology*, 6 (2): 203-220.

Snively, G. and Corsiglia, J. 2001. Discovering Indigenous Science: Implications for Science Education, *Science Education*, vol. 85, pp. 6-34.

South Africa, 1995. *White Paper on Education and Training*, Government Printer, Pretoria, South Africa.

South Africa Department of Education. 2002. *Revised national curriculum statements Grades R- 9: Technology,* Pretoria: Government Gazette no 443 of 23406.

Southern and Eastern African Trade Information and Negotiations Institute (SEATINI), 2001. The selfish interpretation of the convention on biological biodiversity by the University of Lausanne, Switzerland, Vol. 4, No. 05 & 06, 15 & 30 March 2001, *International South Group Network* (ISGN), Harare, Zimbabwe.

Stiglitz, J. 1998. Oped article, In *International Herald Tribune*, October 6, 1998, USA.

Tatira, L. 2000. The Role of *Zviera* in Socialisation, In E. Chiwome, Z. Mguni, & M. Furusa (Eds.), *Indigenous Knowledge and Technology in African and Diasporan Communities,* (pp. 146-151). Harare: University of Zimbabwe.

Taylor, B. & De Loë, R. C. 2012. Conceptualizations of local knowledge in collaborative environmental governance, *Geoforum* 43, pp. 1207–17.

Tempels, P. 1945. *Bantu Philosophy,* Presence Africaine: Paris

Thomas, A. 2004. 'The Study of Development', *Paper prepared for DSA Annual Conference,* 6 November, Church House, London.

Trompenaars, F. 1994. *Riding the waves of culture: Understanding cultural diversity in global business,* Irwin, New York.

Tsiko, S. 2012. 'How the West is bleeding Africa', *The Herald Newspaper,* Harare: Zimbabwe (2 August 2012).

Turnbull, D. 2000. *Masons, tricksters and cartographers: Comparative studies in the sociology of scientific and indigenous knowledge,* Routledge: London.

UNESCO. 2006. *Strategy of Education for Sustainable Development in Sub-Saharan Africa,* UNESCO/BREDA, UNESCO Regional Office for Education in Africa: Paris.

Vandeleur, S. 2010. *Indigenous technology and culture in the technology curriculum: Starting the conversation*, Unpublished PhD Thesis, Rhodes University, South Africa.

Veitayaki, J. 2002. Taking advantage of indigenous knowledge: The Fiji case, *International Social Science Journal*, Vol. 54 (173): 395-402.

Vilakazi, H. W. 1999. The problem of African Universities, In Makgoba, M. W. (Ed). *African Renaissance*, Mafube – Tafelberg: Cape Town, South Africa.

Visvanathan, S. 2009. *The search for cognitive justice*. A seminar presented by the author, in May 2009. Available:http://www.india-seminar.com/2009/597/597shiv visvanathan.htm.

Waite, G. 2000. Traditional medicine and the quest for national identity in Zimbabwe, *Zambezia*, Vol. XXVII (11): 235-268.

Warren, D. M. 1991. *Using indigenous knowledge in agricultural development*. Washington, DC: The World Bank.

Warren, D. M. 1992. 'Indigenous knowledge, Biodiversity Conservation and Development', *Keynote Address at International Conference on Conservation of Biodiversity in Africa: Local Initiatives and Institutional Roles*, Nairobi, Kenya August 30 - September 3, 1992.

Wa Thiongo, N. 1986. *Decolonising the Mind: The politics of Language in African Literature,* Heinemann: Portsmouth, UK.

Wild, H. and Gelfand, M., 1959. Some native herbal remedies at present in use in Mashonaland, *Central African Journal of Medicine* 5 (1959): 292-305.

World Commission on Environment and Development (WCED), 1987. *Our Common Future, Oxford University Press: Oxford.*

World Bank, 1997. Knowledge and Skills for the Information Age, *The First Meeting of the Mediterranean Development Forum*; Mediterranean Development Forum.

World Bank, 1998/99. *World Development Report 1998/1999: Knowledge for Development,* Washington: USA.

World Bank, 1998. Indigenous knowledge for development: A framework for action (Nov 4, 1998), *Knowledge and Learning Centre-African Region*, USA. Available at: http://www.worldbank.org/afr/ik/ikrept.pdf (Accessed: 4 October 2013).

World Bank, 2004. *Indigenous knowledge: Local pathways to global development,* Knowledge and Learning Group-Africa Region.

Xaba, T. 2008. Marginalised medical practice: The marginalisation and transformation of indigenous medicines in South Africa. In *Another knowledge is possible:*

Beyond Northern epistemologies. Ed. Boaventura de Sousa, S. Verso: London. Pp. 317-351. Online version available @ http://www.ces.uc.pt/emancipa/research/en/ft/triunfo. html.

Zerouki, B. 1993. Etude relative au feu aupms des populations des bassins versants types du Haut Niger. *Report Conakry*: République de Guinée: programme d'Aménagement des Bassins Versants Types du Haut Niger.

Zimbabwe Resource Centre for Indigenous Knowledge (ZIRCIK), Harare, Zimbabwe.